As the true head of His church,

God Himself will lead

your ministry as you yield fully to

THE POWER
OF THE CALL

HENRY T. BLACKABY
AND HENRY BRANDT
WITH KERRY L. SKINNER

BROADMAN
&HOLMAN
PUBLISHERS

Nashville, Tennessee

THE POWER

OF THE CALL

© 1997
by Henry T. Blackaby, Henry Brandt, and Kerry L. Skinner
All rights reserved
Printed in the United States of America

0-8054-6297-X

Published by Broadman & Holman Publishers, Nashville, Tennessee
Acquisitions and Development Editor: John Landers

Dewey Decimal Classification: 253
Subject Heading: PASTORAL WORK
Library of Congress Card Catalog Number: 97-11964

Unless otherwise stated, all Scripture citation is from the New King James Version, © 1979, 1980, 1982, Thomas Nelson, Inc., Publishers. Other passages are marked AMP, The Amplified Bible, Old Testament © 1962, 1964 by Zondervan Publishing House, used by permission, and the New Testament © The Lockman Foundation 1954, 1958, 1987, used by permission; NIV, the Holy Bible, New International Version, © 1973, 1978, 1984 by International Bible Society; PHILLIPS, reprinted with permission of Macmillan Publishing Co., Inc. from J. B. Phillips: The New Testament in Modern English, revised edition, © J. B. Phillips 1958, 1960, 1972; and Williams New Testament, The New Testament in the Language of the People, by Charles B. Williams, © 1937, 1966, 1986 by Holman Bible Publishers, used by permission.

Library of Congress Cataloging-in-Publication Data

Blackaby, Henry T., 1935–
    The power of the call / Henry T. Blackaby, Henry Brandt, Kerry L. Skinner.
      p. cm.
    ISBN 0-8054-6297-X (hc)
    1. Clergy—Office. 2. Pastoral theology. I. Brandt, Henry R. II. Skinner, Kerry L., 1955– .
BV660.2.B53   1997
253—dc21

                    97-11964
                    CIP

97 98 99 00 01 5 4 3 2 1

To the many pastors and leaders who have sincerely responded to God's call and who earnestly seek to be God's very best in a hurting world.

and

To our own children who have responded to this call!
HENRY T. BLACKABY

To pastors and staff members who have been instrumental in teaching me how to walk with God.
HENRY BRANDT

With sincere appreciation to all those who have prayed for me while preparing this book and to my wife, Elaine, who is a daily encourager for me.
KERRY L. SKINNER

Contents

Introduction

God has staked a lot on the lives of pastors and the people they lead. His eternal purposes have been entrusted to pastors, to manage His "treasure" (Exod. 19:5), and to respond obediently as He instructs and guides His people on His mission to redeem a lost world. Eternity is at stake! God has also fully provided for every situation and need a pastor will face, and has made available to him

an abundance for every good work.

2 COR. 9:8

Nothing is missing! All is present and available to every pastor-steward of God's people. But many may have lost sight of the nature of their calling and of God's incredible resources. This is why this book has been written—to help pastors and others involved in leading God's people to

- stand before God and His Word and understand in a fresh way the nature of our call;
- meditate on the greatness of the God who called us and the implications of His greatness for our ministry;
- know how to receive all God has provided for us as we serve His people;
- know and experience once again, the joy of our calling in the presence and power of God working in us and through us to the maturing of God's people and the redeeming of a lost world.

The approach of this book is very different from other books written for pastors. It is not a book of methods, though it includes many practical helps. It is a book about relationships—relationships to God and to His people and to the many who will seek us for help because they know we are God's ambassadors and because God Himself will entrust them to us.

1

TWO POINTS OF VIEW

This book is written from two different but crucial points of view. One point of view is from a layman—a professional counselor for fifty-plus years and a faithful, participating church member who has always loved pastors, missionaries, and all of God's people. He has consistently sought to be a friend and enabler of all of those people to be God's best. This view is from Henry Brandt.

The second point of view is from one who has been a pastor for almost thirty years. He is known as a friend and guide to pastors and those who are stewards of God's people. His life has touched leaders of all levels as he has traveled worldwide in helping believers. This view is from Henry T. Blackaby.

Both have experienced what they share. They have a great empathy for pastors and leaders and for the church. They are now actively involved in helping Christians to be fully available to God in a most needy time.

Both authors have noticed that pastors and other church leaders are under great stress. Many are experiencing what they call "burnout"— some being so discouraged and disheartened that they are leaving the ministry. Too many are experiencing great stress in their families and their marriages. Many are utterly bewildered. They know they have been called of God. They know from Scripture the tremendous resources of God; yet they have lost their joy in ministry. They are not seeing much success from their labors, and an increasing number are going through great brokenness as they experience forced termination.

ANSWERS TO THE QUESTIONS PASTORS ASK

In general, pastors are asking several critical questions:

- What is happening?
- What do I do?
- How did I come to this?
- Is there any hope for me or my ministry?
- Is there anywhere I can turn to gain real, practical help?
- How do I return to real joy and fulfillment in my life, my marriage, my family, and my ministry?

The truths shared in this book will indeed help a person find real answers to these questions. This book is not mere theory or quick-fix answers. It is not filled with clichés or flashy proposals. Here, with God's help a person can confront himself, his relationship to God, and God's revealed provisions for his life. Here a pastor can confront real, specific choices he can make that God will honor to bring him to God's fullness of life. Jesus said,

> **I have come that they may have life, and that they may have it more abundantly.**
>
> JOHN 10:10

Paul stated,

> **To know the love of Christ which passes knowledge; that you may be filled with all the fullness of God. Now to Him who is able to do exceedingly abundantly above all that we ask or think, according to the power that works in us.**
>
> EPH. 3:19–20

> **That their hearts may be encouraged, being knit together in love, and attaining to all riches of the full assurance of understanding, to the knowledge of the mystery of God, both of the Father and of Christ, in whom are hidden all the treasures of wisdom and knowledge.**
>
> COL. 2:2–3

May God Himself enable you as you begin a constant pursuit of God. He has said,

> **And you will seek Me and find Me, when you search for Me with all your heart.**
>
> JER. 29:13

This follows a certain promise from God:

> **For thus says the LORD: After seventy years are completed at Babylon, I will visit you and perform My good word toward you, and cause you to return to this place.**
>
> JER. 29:10

Jesus gave this same promise:

> **Ask, and it will be given to you; seek, and you will find; knock, and it will be opened to you.**
>
> MATT. 7:7

And the apostle Paul out of the depth of his own personal experience said,

> **For all the promises of God in Him are Yes, and in Him Amen, to the glory of God through us.**
>
> 2 COR. 1:20

> **Now thanks be to God who always leads us in triumph in Christ, and through us diffuses the fragrance of His knowledge in every place. For we are to God the fragrance of Christ among those who are being saved and among those who are perishing.**
>
> 2 COR. 2:14–15

> **And God is able to make all grace abound toward you, that you, always having all sufficiency in all things, may have an abundance for every good work.**
>
> 2 COR. 9:8

Paul's encouragement to the stewards of God's people is practical, certain, and real.

It would be of great encouragement also to read quietly through John 17 and see not only how Jesus "perfected" His disciples to fulfill God's purposes through them, but to get a firm grasp on what He is right now doing for each of us.

GOD'S PLUMB LINES FOR HIS SERVANTS

Finally, this book is not designed to put down anyone, or any other approach to ministry. Rather, it is to examine the "plumb lines of God" for His servants, and be a guide away from anything that is hurting us or our ministry and into the fullness of joy in God's clear pattern for ministry!

May God help you to experience just that. With an open heart and a heartcry to God, pursue Him as you study this book. You will see God's perspective on your life and ministry through a seasoned layman's eyes and heart and also through a seasoned pastor's eyes and heart. We chose not to mix or blur the two, but rather let you sit with each personally and let us share our hearts with you.

Henry T. Blackaby, Henry Brandt, and Kerry L. Skinner

PART ONE

God's Standard
for Your Calling

ONE

The Role of the Pastor

> *He . . . chose David His servant,*
> *And took him from the sheepfolds; . . .*
> *To shepherd Jacob His people,*
> *And Israel His inheritance.*
> *So he shepherded them according to the integrity of his heart,*
> *And guided them by the skillfulness of his hands.*
> PSALM 78:70–72
>
> *Be careful to preach faithfully the Word of God; pray earnestly for each of the members, and especially to seek the assistance of the Holy Spirit as you pray; love people deeply as you would your Lord; seek earnestly the "fruit of the Spirit"; and function always with a deep sense of stewardship of the people of God, whom He purchased with His own blood and loves as His treasured possession.*
> HENRY T. BLACKABY

HENRY T. BLACKABY

GOD CHOOSES HIS SERVANTS

There were special circumstances surrounding the choosing and the calling of David to be God's servant. God's people had Saul to lead them, but Saul was rejected by the Lord because he failed to obey God. Integrity with God is essential for the life God blesses and uses. Since Saul failed this requirement, God looked for someone He could trust, someone who would love Him and obey Him. God chose David, a shepherd boy, to be king. The most unlikely choice of man was God's choice. People tend to look at the physical appearance, but listen to the words of Scripture:

> **But the LORD said to Samuel, "Do not look at his appearance or at his physical stature, because I have refused him. For the Lord does not see as man sees; for man looks at the outward appearance, but the LORD looks at the heart."**
>
> 1 SAM. 16:7

Through His servant Samuel, God announced to King Saul,

> **But now your kingdom shall not continue. The Lord has sought for Himself a man after His own heart, and the Lord has commanded him to be commander over His people, because you have not kept what the Lord commanded you.**
>
> 1 SAM. 13:14

The Psalms give a more complete picture of that moment:

> **He . . . chose David His servant,**
> **And took him from the sheepfolds; . . .**
> **To shepherd Jacob His people,**
> **And Israel His inheritance.**
> **So he shepherded them according to the integrity of his heart,**
> ***And guided them by the skillfulness of his hands.***
>
> PS. 78:70–72

Here is a clear picture of the one God chooses to guide His people:

- The pastor is *chosen*.
- He is chosen by *God*.
- He is chosen by God to be *His servant*.
- He is chosen by God to *shepherd* His people.
- He recognizes that God's people are His *inheritance*, that they are God's "special treasure" (Exod. 19:5–6).
- He has integrity of heart. (This was foundational to David's assignment from God.)
- He recognizes that his assignment will require "skillfulness of his hands" (hard work, consistent with his heart).

GOD CALLS HIS SERVANTS TO BE STEWARDS

The pastor's role is that of manager or steward of what belongs to God. Pastors are not owners of the flock. The flock is God's. God is the owner; pastors are the managers. This is how Paul instructed the pastors (elders) of the church at Ephesus:

> **Therefore take heed to yourselves and to all the flock, among which the Holy Spirit has made you overseers, to shepherd the church of God which He purchased with His own blood.**
>
> ACTS 20:28

What a poignant illustration of how God instructs those to whom He entrusts His people. Paul continued to use the shepherd image to show the watchcare over the flock:

> **For I know this, that after my departure savage wolves will come in among you, not sparing the flock. Also from among yourselves men will rise up, speaking perverse things, to draw away the disciples after themselves. Therefore watch.**
>
> ACTS 20:29–31

Jesus also used other terms to describe the role of pastor, or one entrusted with the care of what belongs to God. In John 15, Jesus is the vine, but God is the vinedresser. In other parables, God is the owner who entrusts His fields and goods to His servants and then returns to gather what is His.

Being entrusted with what belongs to God, purchased with His own blood, requires careful and studied stewardship. Why? Because God has set a day of accounting. This accounting will always remain on the sensitive steward's heart, for he must always please the One who called him and trusted him.

Jesus said to Peter,

> **Feed My lambs. . . . Tend My sheep. . . . Feed My sheep. . . . Follow Me.**
>
> JOHN 21:15–19

He also commanded all of the disciples with these words:

Make disciples of all the nations, . . . teaching them to observe all things that I have commanded you.

MATT. 28:19–20

A pastor is an undershepherd, for he works under the Great Shepherd, our Lord Jesus. Jesus is the pastor's model, to whom the pastor is accountable. The pastor is to please Him in all the ways he cares for Christ's people. All that Jesus did, when entrusted by the Father with the disciples, will be the task of the pastor with those entrusted to his care. The pastor will love them, even to the laying down of his life for the sheep (1 John 3:16; John 13:34–35; 15:16–17).

GOD CALLS HIS SERVANTS TO BE SPIRITUAL LEADERS

We too often turn to the world for leadership. The tragedy of our day is to search out all the latest books to learn how to be a worldly leader in the life of the church. If you are to lead the people of God, you must be a *spiritual* leader. You cannot do Kingdom work with the world's methods. They do not correlate.

> *You cannot do Kingdom work with the world's methods.*

Kingdom citizens have a completely different set of qualities about their lives. That is especially true of leaders. The changes taking place in our world will continue to come much more rapidly than they did in previous years. While no person can predict the future, there is One who does know what tomorrow holds—God. Do you think next year will catch God off guard? No! He is orchestrating what will happen in many areas of life.

Do you suppose that God wants to develop you so that your life will represent the kind of leader God is looking for? Yes! God has taken upon Himself the responsibility to equip you and prepare you to be the person He works through.

In Genesis 12 God showed what He would do and what He wanted Abraham to do. If Abraham would walk obediently with Him, God would develop his character to match his assignment and make Abraham's name great. A person's name was his character. It was God's responsibility to put in place in Abraham's character everything needed to accomplish what God wanted.

Jesus told the disciples their task was to follow Him. God then began to shape and mold their life and character into what He had in mind when He called them. God is still doing that with believers today. He has been doing that since before the foundation of the world.

Every generation has said that the coming years would be unlike any other time in history. Because of that, every spiritual generation called for a different kind of spiritual leader. We need not a different kind than what Jesus had in mind, but a different kind than we have been seeing.

You can see the qualities that your life needs as Jesus, in you, shapes and molds your life to be the instrument He can work through for your generation. This is evident in the intensity of the life of Jesus as He saw the multitudes:

> **Then Jesus went about all the cities and villages, teaching in their synagogues, preaching the gospel of the kingdom, and healing every sickness and every disease among the people. But when He saw the multitudes, He was moved with compassion for them, because they were weary and scattered, like sheep having no shepherd. Then He said to His disciples, "The harvest truly is plentiful, but the laborers are few. Therefore pray the Lord of the harvest to send out laborers into His harvest."**
>
> MATT. 9:35–38

As you read of the need for spiritual leaders in this passage, you recognize that the urgency of the hour was great—yes, even as it is in our day. Jesus saw a desperate need for a shepherd. He was not looking at the people as Romans or as Gentiles. Jesus was moved with compassion for the people of God.

Pastor, you need to let your heart be absolutely transparent before God about your compassion for His people. When you see them stumbling, fainting, and harassed, your heart will turn upside down. You will suffer with your people when they hurt if you have a shepherd's heart.

Many pastors have no emotional ties with the people they lead. They do not suffer with the people. They keep themselves at a distance and use the people to accomplish a ministry goal.

> *The people* are *your ministry, not the means you use to fulfill your ministry.*

Pastor, do you talk about "my" ministry? The people *are* your ministry, not the means you use to fulfill your ministry. *Your ministry is fulfilled when the people of God become what God intended each one of them to be.* Your goal is to lead them into the fullest possible victorious Christian life that will be observable, believable, transparent, with integrity before God.

Requirements of a Spiritual Leader

1. A leader has an absolute sense of urgency (Matt. 9:35–37). He recognizes the sense of urgency over the condition of God's people. Because of this desperate condition of the sheep (God's people), Jesus sent the disciples on mission to help them.

2. A leader has an absolute priority and commitment to prayer (Matt. 9:38). There is no possibility of a person being a spiritual leader who does not understand the absolute priority and urgency of being a person of prayer. Prayer is a relationship with God where, in His Presence, He reveals who He is and what He is about. You then can have a sensitive heart that reaches out to God, requesting what He has already put on your heart to do.

3. A leader is unconditionally related to Jesus Christ as Lord (Matt. 10:1). Jesus had access to call the Twelve and to do with them what the Father wanted. We must not be sidetracked from the relationship. The slightest whisper from the leader's Lord is heard and responded to immediately. This must be the only call the leader will hear.

4. A leader dwells with and under Christ's absolute spiritual authority and demonstrates this in his life (Matt. 10:1, 8). Jesus does not release His authority; He *is* the leader's authority. Some leaders do not think they can have an absolute word from God. One pastor said, "I don't have an absolute but an impression from God." The world does not need an impression; the world needs an authoritative word straight from the heart of God.

5. A leader is Kingdom oriented (Matt. 6:33). Too often we are so oriented to the world that we are disoriented to the kingdom of God. This is the present rule of a real king. The Lord Jesus rules triumphantly

The World Says:	**The Kingdom of Heaven Says:**
1. Pride is important	1. Humility is important
2. Hitch your wagon to a star	2. Jesus is Lord
3. Be successful	3. Be obedient
4. Be a professional	4. Be a servant
5. Compete with one another	5. Serve one another
6. Defend your rights	6. Give away your rights
7. Negotiate for the best deal	7. Obey God's command absolutely
8. Strive for excellence	8. Strive for Christlikeness
9. Save your life	9. Lose your life
10. Affirm self	10. Deny self
11. Activity is important	11. Character is important
12. You don't have to put up with this	12. Take up your cross
13. Live to die	13. Die to live
14. Rule and get to the top	14. A ruler must be chief servant
15. Things will make you happy	15. Character brings joy
16. Advertise to get response	16. If Christ is lifted up He will draw all to Himself
17. Provide for a rainy day	17. Trust God's faithfulness in all things
18. Walk by sight	18. Walk by faith
19. Set your own goals and priorities	19. The Father alone has the right to set your goals and priorities
20. Take the initiative	20. The Father alone holds the initiative
21. Plan by objectives	21. The Father has His own objectives
22. Befriend the world to reach the world	22. He who is a friend of the world is an enemy of God
23. Hate your enemies	23. Love your enemies

Table 1.1

right now. The Kingdom is for the present experience of those who believe Him and relate to Him. Jesus' message was on the Kingdom and so we must be Kingdom leaders. We must recognize the reigning activity of the living Lord around us.

You cannot do Kingdom work with the world's principles or the world's methods. Look at the radical difference between the Kingdom of heaven and the kingdom of this world.

6. *A leader must be a person of absolute faith and trust (Matt. 10:9–10).*

And God is able to make all grace abound toward you, that you, always having all sufficiency in all things, may have an abundance for every good work.

2 COR. 9:8

7. *A leader lives with a clear sense of God-given direction (Matt. 10:5–7, 11–16).* He knows the ways of God in the world. He is sent with the awareness of the awesome consequences of being sent. Jesus sent His disciples as lambs among wolves. A spiritual leader must not be surprised about what he enters into and experiences.

8. *A leader is clearly committed and aware of the cost involved (Matt. 10:17–23).* People *will* oppose you. You are in deep spiritual warfare. You will find conflict in walking with the Lord. But the Lord will give you what you need to say at the right time.

> *A Spiritual Leader does not worry about what others can do but is absolutely concerned about what God can do.*

9. *A leader has a clear commitment to pattern his life after Jesus as the master servant (Matt. 10:24–25).* He does not pattern his life after the generals of the world but after Christ. The identity of Jesus must include Isaiah 53.

10. *A spiritual leader is God-oriented (Matt. 10:26–31).* He is not afraid of others but confident that God will vindicate him; he has a healthy sense of the fear of God. He does not worry about what others can do but is absolutely concerned about what God can do. God-fearing leaders do not get turned aside by the opinions of others. Do we function more by what others say, or by what God says? This leader will not dare to offend God.

11. A leader bears an open witness to everyone of the absolute Lordship of Jesus Christ, especially in the atmosphere of the world (Matt. 10:32–33).

12. A leader must be willing to risk with eyes wide open, unafraid of the opinions of others, ready for spiritual warfare (Matt. 10:34–36).

13. A leader's love for God and His Son exceeds all other loves (Matt. 10:37–39). If you are not willing to forsake family, you are not worthy of Christ.

14. A leader lives out a life of unmistakable identity with Jesus Christ and does so with an eye to the day of accountability (Matt. 10:40–42). There will be a day when we are rewarded according to the works done in the body, whether good or bad.

Moses had a shepherd's sense of accountability and love for the people when he said,

> **Yet now, if You will forgive their sin—but if not, I pray, blot me out of Your book which You have written.**
>
> Exod. 32:32

GOD'S ASSIGNMENT

Several special moments in the life of a pastor need careful attention to show that he is responding to God and His people as a careful steward.

The Shepherd Being Considered by a Church

Here are counsels when you are being considered by a church to become their pastor.

1. Bring your life before the Lord—as His servant. Review carefully the life of our Lord as your pattern. Deny self and take up your cross (whatever it may cost you to help God's people come from where they are as they have been following Him before He entrusts them to you, to where He now would have them go).

2. Pray! With a heart and integrity before the Lord, pray to have no will of your own, no goal of your own, no plan of your own. Pray to have only what God will show you about His heart for His people—and be ready to be a steward of those He may entrust into your care and keeping.

3. Release your will to His, even before He reveals it. He is Lord and will never make a mistake, but He may give you an assignment you had not anticipated.

The Shepherd Considering a Church

Should a church ask you to come before them so they can speak with you about becoming their pastor, there are some things that may be helpful to remember. The size of the church family, salary, facilities, and community should not be your concern. Instead, ask *God-centered* questions, not *self-centered* questions.

- What has God been doing in this place?
- Where has God brought these people for whom His Son died?
- What has God been saying to them?

Pastor, please do not bring *your* program, methods, or vision to the people. Remember that you are the steward and God is the owner! You are called by God to join Him in what He has been doing, and now wants to do through you for them.

The Shepherd's Role in Beginning a New Ministry

Should God call you clearly to join Him in a new ministry, you should consider the following as your role, as their pastor and as His "undershepherd."

1. *God has been working in His people long before He called you there.* Therefore, for the first year, seek clearly to see and understand what God *has been* doing, so that you can be a spiritual catalyst in enabling them to fulfill all God has been placing on their hearts. Do not give the impression, "Now that I have come, God has come!"

2. *God was working with these people under the former pastor before you arrived.* Be careful to remember that what went on before you got there, was not just "the former pastor's work"; it was God's work *through His people, under the shepherd whom God placed over His people before He called you.* If you try to remove what the former pastor did, you may be saying, "God was not doing anything before I came; I must clean house to do *my work.*" But it is God's work you may be removing.

3. *Listen to the people as they express what they honestly believe God has been doing and saying to them.*

4. *Affirm everything you possibly can.*

5. *Honor the Lord Himself who has been doing it all.*

6. Be a "spiritual catalyst" to help bring about the deepest possible experience with the Living Christ. Paul said,

> **Him we preach, warning every man and teaching every man in all wisdom, that we may present every man perfect in Christ Jesus. To this end I also labor, striving according to His working which works in me mightily.**
>
> Col. 1:28–29

7. Be careful to:

- preach faithfully the Word of God;
- pray earnestly for each of the members, and especially to seek the assistance of the Holy Spirit as you pray;
- love people deeply as you would your Lord;
- seek earnestly the "fruit of the Spirit"; and
- function always with a deep sense of stewardship of the people of God, whom He purchased with His own blood and loves as His treasured possession.

Your role, then, as a spiritual catalyst, is to bring all of the people of God He entrusts to you into the fullest possible personal and corporate relationship with the loving Christ, God being your helper. The people are not there to help you be a successful pastor. You are there by divine assignment to work with God to bring His people to their fullest potential in knowing and doing the will of God for His glory. God has given you all the necessary enabling as He did for David and all the others He called. Be a faithful and good servant of your Lord. This will require faithful discipling of every one of His people. The Book of Acts and John 17 are the finest examples of what that means (see chap. 13 on spiritual leaders).

The rest of this book will seek to give you some clear and helpful guidance and encouragement in your desire to be God's called and faithful servant—to His glory.

PROCESS THE MESSAGE

1. How would you describe the plans you have made for what must happen at the church where you have pastored or currently are pastoring?

2. What was the process you walked through in developing that plan?

3. What has attracted your attention the most when considering a move to a new congregation?

4. When you arrived at a new place of service, how did you consider the work of God through His people under the shepherd whom God placed over His people before He called you there?

T W O

The Nature of the Call

> *Him we preach, warning every man and teaching every man in all wisdom, that we may present every man perfect in Christ Jesus. To this end I also labor, striving according to His working which works in me mightily.*
> COLOSSIANS 1:28–29
>
> *In the late 1950s, after immersing myself in the social sciences for eight years, I fled back to the Bible. . . . To my surprise I met hordes of ministers heading for the social sciences.*
> HENRY BRANDT
>
> *One does not choose the ministry! A pastor is chosen. He is chosen by God for God's purposes, in God's time and place, and serves Him in God's ways.*
> HENRY T. BLACKABY

HENRY BRANDT

Before I begin, let it be clear that I am a layman who sits in the pew, a beneficiary of your expertise.

It was a pastor who caused me to consider my ways, who showed me the benefits of inviting Christ into my life, who taught me how to appropriate the resources available to me from God, who challenged me when I wandered away from those resources, and who taught me how to renew my fellowship with God. It was a pastor who taught me to love the Bible and to search it as the blueprint for my life.

It is the church that has provided me with the inspiration, the fellowship, and opportunity for service that has led me into an abundant life.

I believe the church has the greatest potential for meeting people's inner needs in our country and around the world. If this is true, then I am writing to the most important single group of people who have the potential of being useful, helpful, and productive by teaching society how to live happily together.

I did not always appreciate some of my pastors' efforts. At times I deeply resented and resisted their interest in me. They did not pursue me because my response affirmed them as a minister. Rather, they were serving God for my benefit. But their quiet, loving response to my resistance convinced me that I needed to become a servant of the Lord.

THE WORK OF A SPECIALIST

You are the custodian of the most important information in the world. How does that statement grab you? You are a specialist in what God has to say to people through the Bible. Your divine calling far supercedes all other professions. Your presence and impact has eternal consequences in the world. What you say is in God's name and for His sake.

Consider the work of a physician. He thumps you, cuts you, prescribes foul-tasting medicine, interferes with your normal pace of life, and then bills you.

Is it not strange that the physician is one of the best paid and most respected persons in the community? This is true even though his work is painful and disagreeable to the patient. Your need determines his diagnosis and treatment. He does not tell you what you would like to hear. He tells you what you need to hear. You may wish you could do without the process, but your health depends on his work and your cooperation.

DIAGNOSIS

We need to remind ourselves of the nature of the Bible. One side is expressed like this:

> **But whoever keeps His word, truly the love of God is perfected in him. By this we know that we are in Him.**
>
> 1 JOHN 2:5

Great peace have those who love Your law,
And nothing causes them to stumble.

Ps. 119:165

But he who looks into the perfect law of liberty and contin-
ues in it, and is not a forgetful hearer but a doer of the work,
this one will be blessed in what he does.

JAMES 1:25

The other side is expressed like this:

Whoever commits sin also commits lawlessness, and sin is
lawlessness.

1 JOHN 3:4

"And this is the condemnation, that the light has come into
the world, and men loved darkness rather than light, because
their deeds were evil. For everyone practicing evil hates the
light and does not come to the light, lest his deeds should be
exposed."

JOHN 3:19–20

Have you ever been walking along a road at night and suddenly headlights from an oncoming car blind you? Your reflex action is to turn away. It takes a while to adjust your eyes to the light. Exposure to the Bible is like adjusting your eyes to light.

Jesus said that people are condemned (guilty) because their deeds are evil. The diagnosis of evil is shocking and disturbing, like the announcement that you need an operation.

The dentist, lawyer, accountant, professor, and counselor all do things for us as disagreeable as some of the techniques of the physician. Their work involves helping us face up to poor choices and mistakes, or forcing us to face new horizons. Their work is determined by our needs. These professionals, too, must tell us what we need to hear rather than what we want to hear.

The work of a minister is no more agreeable than the work of these other specialists. It requires the sometimes painful diagnosis of sin, urging unwilling people to repentance and humble acceptance of the cleansing available only from God. The process involves declaring

God's standards. The needs and deeds of people determine the minister's message. The pastor understands the process. It may be disagreeable and disturbing, but the result is peace.

Some people accept the physician's diagnosis, and some do not. Some people accept the pastor's diagnosis, and some do not. In either case, the diagnosis is hard to take, and the work is not easy.

Let's take a look at another familiar passage, Hebrews 4:12:

> **For the word of God is living and powerful, and sharper than any two-edged sword, piercing even to the division of soul and spirit, and of joints and marrow, and is a discerner of the thoughts and intents of the heart.**

Because the Word of God is sharp, piercing, and discerning, it takes a kind, loving, gentle preacher to deliver the Word. How can the diagnosis of sin and evil become a happy, cheery, delightful experience? I know of no way. The process is hard to take. It is the *result* that is happy, cheery, and delightful. The process leads people to the resources of God. What a high calling!

> *Because the Word of God is sharp, piercing, and discerning, it takes a kind, loving, gentle preacher to deliver the Word.*

The question has been put to me, "You have not made much reference to psychology. Are you not sold on your field?"

Well, a simple definition of psychology would be that it is a study of people and what makes them tick. As far as I am concerned, I have not found a more effective sourcebook to describe people and find solutions to their needs than the Scriptures.

Contemporary psychology does not recognize God. When you expose yourself to this field, you are exposing yourself to people who, almost entirely, do not take the Bible into account. In fact, there will be a good deal of pressure put on you in your counseling not to bring your biblical views into the conversation. I do not see how a Christian has any alternative but to declare the truths of the Bible if a person has deviated from them. I am grateful that my pastors corrected me.

Some people would say very critically that a minister has a Scripture verse for everything. But what is wrong with that? A Christian should listen and speak on the basis of his working biblical knowledge. Deviation from that standard is not in our own best interests. If the pastor wants to have a redemptive relationship with people, he must make it very clear that the basis for diagnosing righteousness and evil is the Bible. Eventually, all people must compare themselves to this standard. Yes, that is rigid, but it is the basis upon which we will be judged one day. The Bible tells us

> **Blessed is the man**
> **who does not walk in the counsel of the wicked**
> **or stand in the way of sinners or sit in the seat of mockers.**
> **But his delight is in the law of the LORD, and on his law he**
> **meditates day and night.**
>
> Ps. 1:1–2, NIV

STAY FOCUSED ON SCRIPTURE

If I were the devil I would try to get all the preachers in the country to meditate on something else besides the Bible. I would make them think that the important thing is to have a roomful of books—the more books the more insight you will have as a minister.

Note: The person who does not know the Bible simply does not know what he does not know. The Bible points the way. If you will follow that way, you will be blessed. If you are not blessed, it is because you have deviated from the way.

In college and graduate school I was knowingly, deliberately, consciously, and openly biased. (You are not supposed to be a student and be biased.) I started out my studies on the premise that the Bible is true. That meant several things. It meant that when I read a book, the book was on trial, not the Bible. When I listened to a lecture, the lecture was on trial, not the Bible.

The person who does not know the Bible simply does not know what he does not know.

I cannot understand the difference between a bias that rules the Bible out and a bias that rules the Bible in. Why are you more scientific because you elect to rule the Bible out than if you elect to rule the Bible in?

"How do you know the Bible is true?" I answer that very simply. I do not know that it is true. I simply accept it by faith. "What if you are wrong?" I do not consider it any challenge to defend the Bible. I have been using the Bible for fifty years, and I can point to a long trail of people that have received help by my listening to their stories and exposing them to the Bible.

> *Sadly the voice of the pastor calling people to repent of their sins and walk in the Spirit gets weaker and weaker.*

In the late 1950s, after immersing myself in the social sciences for eight years, I fled back to the Bible. I knew the Bible was the only basis for guiding people to a redemptive relationship with God. To my surprise I met hordes of ministers heading for the social sciences.

Sadly the voice of the pastor calling people to repent of their sins and walk in the Spirit gets weaker and weaker. The call to get help to live with our sins gets louder and louder.

Some ministers tell me that people are uncomfortable in their presence. Perhaps. It is imperative that the minister is comfortable in his role. The minister should be able to stand tall and let it be known that the listeners are in the presence of someone who has been totally changed by a relationship to Jesus Christ and His Word.

My message to the minister is to go back to the Bible. My voice seems too weak.

Listen and you will hear a Voice that is like thunder before a refreshing rain.

HENRY T. BLACKABY

THE PASTOR: WHO HE IS

One does not choose the ministry! A pastor is chosen. He is chosen by God for God's purposes, in God's time and place, and serves Him in

God's ways. God has chosen to change others and our world through pastors who are called by God, who answer this call, and who obey God consistently. God has chosen to bring both His people and the pastor to "fullness of life." He does this by expressing Himself—His presence and power—*in* the pastor and *through* the Scriptures.

No one else in society has a greater or higher calling; no one else can see so great a difference made in the lives of individuals, homes, and workplaces. The pastor and the people of God are God's great gift of love to a broken and hurting world.

Yet everything depends on how one views, understands, and responds to this "upward call of God in Christ Jesus" (Phil. 3:14). The understanding of this call determines how a person lives and functions; but this understanding must come from the Scriptures. A thorough picture of the call is found in Paul's letter to the church at Rome:

> **Paul, a bondservant of Jesus Christ, called to be an apostle, separated to the gospel of God which He promised before through His prophets in the Holy Scriptures, concerning His Son Jesus Christ our Lord, who was born of the seed of David according to the flesh, and declared to be the Son of God with power according to the Spirit of holiness, by the resurrection from the dead. Through Him we have received grace and apostleship for obedience to the faith among all nations for His name, among whom you also are the called of Jesus Christ.**
>
> ROM. 1:1–6

This is an incredible call, unequaled by any other vocation in the world! It is simple and straightforward.

THE CALL OF GOD

This call is not by the will of man, but "by the will of God" (Eph. 1:1; 2 Tim. 1:1).

> **Paul, an apostle (not from men nor through man, but through Jesus Christ and God the Father who raised Him from the dead).**
>
> GAL. 1:1

Paul, an apostle of Jesus Christ by the will of God, and Timothy our brother.

Col. 1:1

God Himself, the Creator of the universe, is the One who saw the need to call pastors. God, the Redeemer of all. God, the Sustainer of everything that is. God, the Sovereign over all time and eternity. He, Himself, is the One who initiates and implements this call. God chooses to place a pastor in a special relationship with Himself and with Jesus Christ. God placed all of Himself in Christ (Col. 2:9), and thereby placed all His fullness in us (2:10).

The One who called us, is Lord of lords, King of kings, the Alpha and Omega—the One who begins all things and completes all things.

"For I am God, and there is no other; I am God, and there is none like Me."

Isa. 46:9

> *The one God calls, He enables by His presence to fulfill completely his call. Any other assignment offered by the world will always be a huge step down!*

This is the God who personally calls His servants: Abraham, Moses, the prophets, the disciples, Paul, Martin Luther, John Wesley, Hudson Taylor—and you and I. We do not deserve it, nor are we capable to handle such a calling. Our call affects others—even to nations and history itself. The one God calls, He enables by His presence to fulfill completely his call. Any other assignment offered by the world will always be a huge step down!

In recent years I have watched many people diminish the sacredness of God's specific call to be a shepherd to His people. We heard people say, "Everyone is called." But in the Scriptures, God specifically calls some to shepherd His people. The call and the enabling are special. Do not let anyone explain away your high calling, and make it common to all. It is not common!

RESOURCES OF THE CALL

In this calling, God makes us

ambassadors for Christ, as though God were pleading through us.

2 COR. 5:20

He makes available to us, and through us, all the resources of God:

For all the promises of God in Him are Yes, and in Him Amen, to the glory of God through us.

2 COR. 1:20

And God is able to make all grace abound toward you, that you, always having all sufficiency in all things, may have an abundance for every good work.

2 COR. 9:8

As His divine power has given to us all things that pertain to life and godliness, through the knowledge of Him who called us by glory and virtue, by which have been given to us exceedingly great and precious promises, that through these you may be partakers of the divine nature, having escaped the corruption that is in the world through lust.

2 PET. 1:3–4

So Jesus said to them, " . . . I say to you, if you have faith as a mustard seed, you will say to this mountain, 'Move from here to there,' and it will move; and nothing will be impossible for you."

MATT. 17:20–21

What then shall we say to these things? If God is for us, who can be against us? He who did not spare His own Son, but delivered Him up for us all, how shall He not with Him also freely give us all things? . . . Yet in all these things we are more than conquerors through Him who loved us. For I am persuaded that neither death nor life, nor angels nor principalities nor powers, nor things present nor things to come, nor height nor depth, nor any other created thing, shall be able to separate us from the love of God which is in Christ Jesus our Lord. (Rom. 8:31–32, 37–39).

There is no doubt that all God's resources are at the disposal of the one whom God has called. These resources are more than sufficient! Jesus said, "If you have faith as a mustard seed, nothing will be impossible for you" (Matt. 17:20).

God Himself is your resource. He enables every pastor to be a channel of His presence and power to the lives of others. This is clearly the witness of Matthew 10, as Jesus enabled the disciples to see God make life-changing differences in others' lives. Paul described God's call by saying,

> **But by the grace of God I am what I am, and His grace toward me was not in vain; but I labored more abundantly than they all, yet not I, but the grace of God which was with me.**
>
> 1 COR. 15:10

> **I have been crucified with Christ; it is no longer I who live, but Christ lives in me; and the life which I now live in the flesh I live by faith in the Son of God, who loved me and gave Himself for me. I do not set aside the grace of God; for if righteousness comes through the law, then Christ died in vain.**
>
> GAL. 2:20–21

Pastor, your call and your enabling are from God. You are God's precious presence to hear and bless in any place where God assigns you.

THE MESSAGE OF THE CALL

Significant is God's message, delivered by the pastor and given to God's people, and to the broken and hurting people he and the church will serve. Jesus said

> **that repentance and remission of sins should be preached in His name to all nations.**
>
> LUKE 24:47

What an assignment! To be sent, by God Himself, with the "keys of the kingdom of heaven" (Matt. 16:19), and given the ministry of reconciliation, that is, that God was in Christ reconciling the world to Himself, not imputing their trespasses to them.

2 Cor. 5:18–19

Every pastor can assure anyone, that

where sin abounded, grace abounded much more.

Rom. 5:20

Sin is the source of human hurt and brokenness! A pastor has God's best solution for sin, the full provision to deal with sin, and the power to restore any person immediately to cleanness and wholeness with God and others. For God

made Him who knew no sin to be sin for us that we might become the righteousness of God in Him.

2 Cor. 5:21

No one, in all of society, has such an awesome privilege as a pastor—*called* by God as His ambassador to a lost and dying world, with the resources of God to meet their deepest need.

THE IMPACT OF THE CALL

What then can be the impact of the life of a pastor in our broken world today? It is *immeasurable*! When a pastor lives a life of holiness and obedience, there is no limit to the good God will do through that life. How crucial, then, it is for a pastor to know clearly who he is as a man called by God.

The pastor is to "walk worthy of the calling" with which he was called (Eph. 4:1). His commission has infinite implication, for his Master has given him an assurance:

And Jesus came and spoke to them, saying, "All authority has been given to Me in heaven and on earth. Go therefore and make disciples of all the nations, baptizing them in the name of the Father and of the Son and of the Holy Spirit, teaching them to observe all things that I have commanded you; and lo, I am with you always, even to the end of the age." Amen.

Matt. 28:18–20

Again, included in this awesome assignment was the promise of all the resources of God:

> **"But you shall receive power when the Holy Spirit has come upon you; and you shall be witnesses to Me in Jerusalem, and in all Judea and Samaria, and to the end of the earth."**
>
> ACTS 1:8

No one else, in all of society today, can claim such an assignment. No one else has such resources to accomplish this task. No wonder laymen anticipate so much from a pastor, with a rightful expectation! Paul pleaded,

> **We then, as workers together with Him also plead with you not to receive the grace of God in vain.**
>
> 2 COR. 6:1

THE ACCOUNTABILITY IN THE CALL

There is no doubt God will hold every pastor accountable for the incredible measure of grace provided for ministry. Paul, again, knew this and said,

> **Therefore we make it our aim, whether present or absent, to be well pleasing to Him. For we must all appear before the judgment seat of Christ, that each one may receive the things done in the body, according to what he has done, whether good or bad. Knowing, therefore, the terror of the Lord, we persuade men; but we are well known to God, and I also trust are well known in your consciences.**
>
> 2 COR. 5:9–11

God announced to Abraham,

> **Abraham shall surely become a great and mighty nation, and all the nations of the earth shall be blessed in him.**
>
> GEN. 18:18

Jesus said to His disciples,

> **You are the salt of the earth; . . . You are the light of the world.**
>
> MATT. 5:13–14

Go into all the world and preach the gospel.
<small>MARK 16:15</small>

And I will give you the keys of the kingdom of heaven, and whatever you bind on earth will be bound in heaven, and whatever you loose on earth will be loosed in heaven.
<small>MATT. 16:19</small>

Could anyone bring such help and blessing to anyone, anywhere, at any time, with such absolute assurance of using all God's resources in the lives of hurting people?

I lived in the midst of utter brokenness while pastoring in California. I experienced God doing everything He said He would in hundreds of broken lives—gangs were saved, murderers saved, marriages healed, homes established. God's presence transformed people and situations that no one else in society could touch.

When I pastored in the San Francisco area, there was much gang activity. One young man resisted the gangs and eventually was caught in a trap. He killed one of the gang members. Police officers laughed when I came to visit the young man. However, I led this man to God's salvation from his jail cell after he had murdered another man. I then conducted the funeral for the slain victim and saw our church share hope and comfort to the grieving families. Twenty-three teenagers came to know the love of Christ at the funeral! All of this happened while many police officers watched. Only God has the resources for those tremendous life-changing experiences.

The world did not have these resources. Our church had to meet these needs. I never referred anyone to the world's resources. I led them to God's resources—and He never failed!

THE REWARD IN THE CALL

Every pastor longs to hear from his Lord,

> **"'Well done, good and faithful servant; you have been faithful over a few things, I will make you ruler over many things. Enter into the joy of your lord.' Then the King will say to those on His right hand, 'Come, you blessed of My Father,**

inherit the kingdom prepared for you from the foundation of the world.'"

MATT. 25:23, 34

A pastor can have the joy of the Lord fill his life daily as he obeys Him and His call. He will have the incredible sense of fulfillment in watching lives and homes, and entire communities, come alive in a fresh encounter with the God who loves them. He can literally see God exchange

beauty for ashes,
The oil of joy for mourning,
The garment of praise for the spirit of heaviness.

ISA. 61:3

What a calling! How exciting it is that all God says is true in real life!

P R O C E S S   T H E   M E S S A G E

1. Where do you get your sense of personal worth?

2. How important is your presence and impact in the world as a pastor?

3. How have you been affected by the world's counsel?

4. How would you compare your study of God's Word versus the time you spend reading other materials?

5. Remember when God called you? How has His call shaped your life?

6. How has God used you to change the lives of others?

7. How have you sought to present every person in your area of influence as "perfect in Christ Jesus" (Col. 1:28)?

8. How would you know if you had finished the task of presenting "every man perfect in Christ Jesus"?

T H R E E

A Reminder of Your Purpose

Our eyes fixed on Jesus the source and goal of our faith. For he himself endured a cross and thought nothing of its shame because of the joy he knew would follow his suffering; and he is now seated at the right hand of God's throne. Think constantly of him enduring all that sinful men could say against him and you will not lose your purpose or your courage.

HEBREWS 12:2–3, PHILLIPS

Pastor, God called you to preach repentance and teach the people of God to observe all things He commanded. Teaching the people of God to live a Spirit-filled life is critical.

HENRY BRANDT

God Himself chose us, called us in His time, and separated us out for Himself. As clearly as God separated from all other days and sanctified the seventh day (set it apart for Himself, Gen. 3:3) and commanded it to be "the Sabbath of the Lord your God" (Exod. 20:10), so God set you apart from all others—for Himself!

HENRY T. BLACKABY

HENRY BRANDT

As I write, it is the Easter season. We color Easter eggs, buy chocolate bunnies, put them in a basket, and give them to little children. The grownups buy a new set of clothes and attend church.

Bringing up the rear is an obscure reason for the season. The school system in my county simply calls it spring break. Teachers are careful not to mention that Jesus was crucified, and in three days, rose from the dead.

In my opinion, Easter is fading as a meaningful Christian holiday.

WHAT IS THE REASON FOR THE SEASON?

My mind goes back to another season—Christmas. Our county school system simply calls it winter break. Christmas time is shopping time. Santa Claus has center stage. He is a merry, benevolent old gentleman. We look at him and the exchange of presents to inspire us to be generous and cheerful. We (except for whoever is stuck in the kitchen) look forward eagerly to the biggest, most enjoyable feast of the year.

Christmas time is the largest alcohol sales week of the year. Christmas parties abound. People wistfully greet each other with a "Merry Christmas." The Bible, one of the best selling and least read books of all time, gives us the true reason for the season. An angel of the Lord said,

> **And she will bring forth a son, and you shall call his name**
> **JESUS, for he will save his people from their sins.**
> **MATT. 1:21**

Isn't it strange? The word sin has all but disappeared out of our vocabularies. Many of us do not know how to define the word. Jesus considered it important. Notice His last words to His disciples before He parted from them and was carried up to heaven:

> **And that repentance and remission of sins should be**
> **preached in His name to all nations, beginning at Jerusalem.**
> **LUKE 24:47**

I like the Phillips translation of the same verse:

> **So must the change of heart which leads to forgiveness of**
> **sins be proclaimed in his name to all nations.**
> **LUKE 24:47, PHILLIPS**

You can be saved from your sinful ways; that is the reason for the Easter season.

There is more to the birth, death, and resurrection of Jesus. A host of angels appeared to some shepherds tending their flocks and announced the birth of Jesus, saying,

> **Glory to God in the highest,**
> **And on earth peace, goodwill toward men!**
> **LUKE 2:14**

Cleaning up our sinful hearts is the doorway to better things. The reason for the Easter season is to remember that the living Savior died to make it possible for us to find a source of peace for our own hearts and goodwill toward all the people who have sinned against us.

In the garden, as He awaited the arrival of Judas with the soldiers who would crucify Him, Jesus said to His Father God,

> **I have glorified You on the earth. I have finished the work which You have given Me to do.**
>
> **JOHN 17:4**

The Bible makes a statement about the crucifixion. It says Jesus endured the cross because of the joy He knew would follow His suffering. He gladly endured the cross. How is that possible?

There is no human remedy for sin. There is no alternate source of a new response to evil deeds.

Jesus did not instruct His disciples to tell the world to remember His suffering and death. That was the price He paid for our sins. He instructed His disciples to tell all nations that if we repent of our sins, we are forgiven on the spot. *This* is the reason for the season.

After Jesus was crucified, His disciples gathered in a room with the doors locked. They were filled with fear. Jesus appeared in the middle of them and said,

> **"Peace to you! As the Father has sent Me, I also send you." And when He had said this, He breathed on them, and said to them, "Receive the Holy Spirit."**
>
> **JOHN 20:21–22**

My mind races to a description of the work of the Holy Spirit in our lives:

> **The Spirit, however, produces in human life fruits such as these: love, joy, peace, patience, kindness, generosity, fidelity, tolerance and self-control.**
>
> **GAL. 5:22–23, PHILLIPS**

This is the reason for the Easter season. We have a source of instant cleansing of our sins—a source that will produce in human life the fruit of the Spirit. There is no human remedy for sin. There is no alternate source of a new response to evil deeds.

Shortly before His arrest, Jesus said to His disciples,

> **He who has My commandments and keeps them, it is he who loves Me. And he who loves Me will be loved by My Father, and I will love him and manifest Myself to him.**
>
> JOHN 14:21

The Lord will not make Himself known to you until you begin to obey His commandments. Before Jesus ascended to heaven, He gave His disciples two directives:

> **"And that repentance and remission of sins should be preached in His name to all nations, beginning at Jerusalem.**
>
> LUKE 24:47

> **Teaching them to observe all things that I have commanded you; and lo, I am with you always, even to the end of the age." Amen.**
>
> MATT. 28:20

Pastor, God called you to preach repentance and teach the people of God to observe all things He commanded. Teaching the people of God to live a Spirit-filled life is critical.

Filled with the Spirit or Filled with Sin?

While my wife and I were researching the subject of sin, we also discovered verses that describe the fruit of the Spirit. Look at the difference living while being filled with the Spirit and in living a "normal" life with sin in control. This chart is from Mark 7:21–23; Romans 1:28–31; Galatians 5:19–21; Ephesians 4:25–31; and 2 Timothy 3:1–5.

As you scan the right-hand column, a Bible verse becomes very meaningful:

> **No man can justify himself before God by a perfect performance of the Law's demands—indeed it is the straight edge of the Law that shows us how crooked we are.**
>
> ROM. 3:20, PHILLIPS

SPIRIT-CONTROLLED LIVING VERSUS SIN-CONTROLLED LIVING

SPIRIT-FILLED MIND

forgiveness	humility
hope	thankfulness
appreciation	confidence
willingness	wisdom
impartiality	faithful
self-control	gratitude
merciful	

SINS OF THE MIND

unforgiveness	pride
evil thoughts	ingratitude
covetousness	selfish ambition
greed	deceitfulness
lust	heartless
arrogance	faithless
senseless	haughty
despiteful	

SPIRIT-FILLED EMOTIONS

love	joy
peace	long-suffering
gentle spirit	kindly spirit
gladness	patient
	compassion

SINFUL EMOTIONS

hatred	anger
rebellion	unloving attitude
bitterness	jealousy
envy	malice
bad temper	rage

SPIRIT-FILLED MOUTH

truthfulness	praise
thankfulness	timeliness
gentle answer	soothing tongue
encouraging	pleasant words
tact	

SINS OF THE MOUTH

lying	slandering
complaining	disputing
yelling	backbiting
contentiousness	quarrelsomeness
boasting	blasphemy
gossip	

SPIRIT-FILLED BEHAVIOR

kindness	gentleness
righteousness	self-control
obedience	cooperation
goodness	sincerity
courage	servant
endurance	submissive
considerate	impartial

SINS OF BEHAVIOR

fornication	brutality
adultery	without self-
drunkenness	control
murder	stealing
revelry	violence
insolent	disobedience to
ruthless	parents
factious	brawling
	favoritism

There is no human remedy that will change our sinful hearts.

There is a human help that will enable you to live with a sinful heart. Teaching, training, and therapy can help you draw upon your willpower and determination. You can learn to be alert to evil thoughts and stirrings of emotions and redirect them constructively. Supervision and being held accountable to someone can help. Drugs can help. Discovering unwholesome attitudes and motivations can help. Setting goals can help. Behavior modification is the best we can do.

But, there is a supernatural way to change the sinful heart. Several Bible verses point the way:

> **"If you openly admit by your own mouth that Jesus Christ is Lord, and if you believe in your own heart that God raised him from the dead you will be saved."**
>
> ROM. 10:9–10, PHILLIPS

> **"And she will bring forth a Son, and you shall call His name Jesus, for He will save His people from their sins."**
>
> MATT. 1:21

> **If we freely admit that we have sinned we find God utterly reliable and straightforward—he forgives our sins and makes us thoroughly clean from all that is evil."**
>
> 1 JOHN 1:9, PHILLIPS

There is then a supernatural miracle available to us.

> **And not only that, but we also glory in tribulations, knowing that tribulation produces perseverance; and perseverance, character; and character, hope. Now hope does not disappoint, because the love of God has been poured out in our hearts by the Holy Spirit who was given to us.**
>
> ROM. 5:3–5

The Spirit produces fruit in human life such as love, joy, peace, patience, kindness, generosity, fidelity, and self-control. There is no human source of such qualities. They are freely available to anyone who has received Jesus Christ as Lord. The key is to

> **Walk in the Spirit, and you shall not fulfill the lust of the flesh.**
>
> GAL. 5:16

You will become gentler, kinder, more patient, more generous, and able to manage your urges so they satisfy you and the people around you. Isn't that what you are looking for?

HENRY T. BLACKABY

It is our very *life*: to return to Christ and therefore the true meaning and significance of Christmas and Easter (and Pentecost, and the final return of Jesus for that matter). Christmas and Easter are not mental suggestions, they are *divine announcements* essential to life, here and now, and for eternity!

If this is true regarding times of the year, how much more is this true concerning your calling by God to the gospel ministry.

The apostle Paul often referred to his moment of call by saying,

Paul, an apostle of Jesus Christ *by the will of God.*
EPH. 1:1, MY EMPHASIS;
SEE ALSO: COL. 1:1; 1 TIM. 1:1;
2 TIM. 1:1; 1 COR. 1:1; 2 COR. 1:1

Paul and Timothy, bondservants of Jesus Christ
PHIL. 1:1

Paul, an apostle (not from men nor through man, but through Jesus Christ and God the Father)
GAL. 1:1

Paul, a bondservant of Jesus Christ, *called to be an apostle*, separated to the gospel of God which He promised before through His prophets in the Holy Scriptures, concerning His Son Jesus Christ our Lord.
ROM. 1:1–3, MY EMPHASIS

God Himself chose us, called us in His time, and separated us for Himself. As clearly as God separated from all other days and sanctified the seventh day (set it apart for Himself, (Gen. 3:3) and commanded it to be "the Sabbath of the LORD your God" (Exod. 20:10), so God set you apart from all others—for Himself! Paul was so deeply affected by God's call on his life that he pleaded with others:

> **We then, as workers together with Him also plead with you not to receive the grace of God in vain.**
>
> 2 COR. 6:1

Paul wanted to remember that

> **we are ambassadors for Christ, as though God were pleading through us.**
>
> 2 COR. 5:20

What an incredible reminder of our purpose! In this context of God's call and claim on our lives, God's statement in Malachi is tremendous:

> **My covenant was with him, one of life and peace.**
> **And people should seek the law from his mouth;**
> **For he is the messenger of the Lord of hosts.**
>
> MAL. 2:5, 7

God's people are the only ones He has assigned to bring everyone into the experience of His salvation and His fullness of life!—this assignment is unique! And when abundant life (John 10:10) begins to be experienced in ever-increasing measure, not only is a life deeply affected, but every life he or she touches is likewise affected for good. Light dispels the darkness, and salt preserves and brings flavor to everything. And even more amazing and exciting is the life of a pastor who has been given the stewardship of God's people, to create an atmosphere of Life and be an enabler of God's people to experience the Life of God in all His fullness in the life of the Church.

Jesus said to His disciples,

> **I have come that they may have life, and that they may have it more abundantly.**
>
> JOHN 10:10

THE GOOD SHEPHERD'S PURPOSE

Jesus said He was the Good Shepherd who would

- Lead them in and out;
- Lead them to green pastures and beside still waters;

- Lead them in the paths of righteousness—for His name's sake;
- Protect them so that, even if they pass through the valley of the shadow of death, they would not need to fear any evil for He would be with them and His rod and staff would comfort them;
- Provide for them so that, if surrounded by enemies, He would set a banquet table before them;
- Continue with them; His mercy and grace would follow them all the days of their lives, and they would never want for any good thing (Ps. 23, John 10).

The life of Jesus made all this real and personal in those who heard His voice and followed Him. What sin had done He came to undo. For those in darkness, they would see a great light. For those in prison, they would be set free. For the blind, they would see. The deaf would hear, and the lame would walk. He Himself was the way, the truth, the life, the water, the bread, the door, and the vine.

SET FREE FROM SIN

For almost thirty years I served God's people as their pastor. No thrill equaled being a part of God setting people free and filling them with unspeakable joy. To literally see the life of God change and fill lives and homes and communities was a tremendous experience.

After many months of loving and sharing with Don, I saw God deliver him from a life of alcohol. God delivered him from bars, prostitutes' rooms, and the edge of suicide. God filled Don's life with His life! Meaning and purpose surged through him. He found joy in marrying a widow in our church. He served as a faithful usher, greeting members and strangers alike. Only God could have brought this about. Don's dear aging and godly mother knew the excitement of her son's returning to God:

> *What God did regularly and faithfully, nothing in society could do, and we knew it well.*

"for this my son was dead and is alive again; he was lost and is found." And they began to be merry.

LUKE 15:24

The whole church and community was filled with joy concerning Don's life. Many were encouraged to seek God's power in their lives too. What God did regularly and faithfully, nothing in society could do, and we knew it well.

THE PASTOR'S PURPOSE

In the first five years of pastoring, I conducted more than three hundred funerals—often in the most tragic of circumstances: drug overdose, murder, suicide, cancer, fatal accidents, little children, youth and those in the prime of life, paupers, city councilmen, family members, and those totally alone. Our church saw God in overwhelming power, comforting, strengthening, giving direction and hope. Many were saved during the funeral or shortly after.

The entire community felt the Presence of God and His love. No one in all of the community could have done what we did, as God's children.

I was constantly reminded of my purpose as a pastor:

1. To bring God's "good news" to a hurting, dying, helpless world.
2. To see people saved and set free from the bondage of sin by God's mighty power.
3. To help new believers experience all God's fullness in ever-increasing measure day after day.
4. To help God's people together to be a living body of Christ in our community, doing in our day what Jesus did in His day.
5. To help us keep our focus on Jesus, seeking always

that I may know Him and the power of His resurrection, and the fellowship of His sufferings, being conformed to His death, if, by any means, I may attain to the resurrection from the dead.

PHIL. 3:10–11

I found that I had to work at keeping my focus on my purpose. It was easy to become primarily involved in administering the organization instead of ensuring that each member was growing in Christ. I could give myself to building buildings instead of building homes and families in the experience of the fullness of God! I could spend time teaching methods rather than teaching "the whole counsel of God" (Acts 20:27). I could spend so much time "counseling" that I would have little or no time for "prayer and the ministry of the word" (Acts 6:4). In the Book of Acts, by the fourth chapter, the men numbered five thousand in the church (v. 4), which meant the church could have numbered twenty to twenty-five thousand! Yet the focus of the apostles was constant:

"But we will give ourselves continually to prayer and to the ministry of the word."

ACTS 6:4

And they continued steadfastly in the apostles' doctrine and fellowship, in the breaking of bread, and in prayers.

ACTS 2:42

They would bear witness to Jesus, with ever-increasing "boldness" in the power and enabling of the Holy Spirit. As a result, the church had boldness in witness.

Then fear came upon every soul.

ACTS 2:43

And many believed and were added to them, and joy and the fullness of God's presence was experienced by all.

Buildings, budgets, committees, planning, and personal counseling are necessary, but they are never primary! God's people and what is happening in their lives is primary, with Christ having preeminence in all things (Col. 1:18).

We hold in our lives what God wants for every person. The world cannot give it; it is ours to share and to enjoy. We must always guard our hearts and lives and never cloud or lose our purpose.

PROCESS THE MESSAGE

1. Read Matthew 1:21 and see why Jesus came.

2. What was the first message of John the Baptist, the forerunner of Jesus?

3. What was the message that Christ preached?

4. What message did Jesus leave before He ascended to heaven?

5. How prominent should the message of repentance be from your pulpit?

6. How much of your time is personally spent developing the people of God in their growth in Christ?

PART TWO

God's Standard for Your Message

FOUR

The Pastor's Message

Then He said to them, "Thus it is written, and thus it was necessary for the Christ to suffer and to rise from the dead the third day, and that repentance and remission of sins should be preached in His name to all nations, beginning at Jerusalem.
LUKE 24:46–47

If a man is a sinner, the diagnosis disturbs him. It is my responsibility and the pastors' to declare the truth to him. It is important we speak the truth in love by describing what he will see in the mirror of God's Word.
HENRY BRANDT

Pastors must deal with the awful reality of sin—sin in their own lives, sin in the people of God, and sin in the multitude of lost people around them. No life or ministry can know victory, success, and joy that ignores the reality of sin and God's solution and provision for sin.
HENRY T. BLACKABY

HENRY BRANDT

Members of my profession have been critical of the church. They say, "We have had clients come to us who have been to your churches. They were upset because they heard messages on the sinfulness of man, and this disturbed them. Preaching about sin is disturbing; therefore, you should not do it. Soothe the people. Many ministers listened and have agreed that certainly we do not want to upset people, and therefore we must seek a more soothing, more satisfying message.

The Pastor's Message Is Not Painless

I have discovered that self-examination is equally incisive when it comes to matters of the Spirit. I have not found a way to make it pleasant. We love darkness rather than light. We tend to justify ourselves, and we shrink from something that tells us what is wrong with us. The truth may be difficult, but this is no reason to withdraw from speaking the truth.

If a man is a sinner, a correct diagnosis disturbs him. It is my responsibility and the pastors' to declare the truth to him. It is important we speak the truth in love by describing what he will see in the mirror of God's Word. Some people go from minister to minister to find one who will tell them what they want to hear. The Scripture states,

> **For the time will come when they will not endure sound doctrine, but according to their own desires, because they have itching ears, they will heap up for themselves teachers; and they will turn their ears away from the truth, and be turned aside to fables.**
>
> 2 Tim. 4:3–4

People Will Resist the Message

A young man was resentful and bitter toward his wife because she opposed his purchase of a sports car. She wanted to spend the money on furniture.

I said to him, "Your bitterness is causing your stomachache. You need a change of heart." People will struggle against that, even though it is true. If it is not true that you are resentful, then I am sorry that I misunderstood you. But if it is true, then you need to repent.

This man and I became locked in opposition. I was using the Bible as a mirror. He did not want to see himself in the mirror. That is human nature. People will resist the truth. If they cannot have their own way, they would rather be unhappy than happy. I have had people say, "Not only am I unhappy, but I want people to know it." How confused can you get, when your goal is to become more touchy and harder to live with?

But there is more to the story. I shared this next verse with the husband:

> **But the wisdom that is from above is first pure, then peaceable, gentle, willing to yield, full of mercy and good fruits, without partiality and without hypocrisy.**
>
> JAMES 3:17

This wisdom comes from *above*, not from choosing the right environment or the proper combination of people. This comes from God. Why did this man not have the wisdom from above in his heart? He did not even want it.

> **Now the fruit of righteousness is sown in peace by those who make peace.**
>
> JAMES 3:18

Where do these qualities come from? Again, from above. They are available to anyone who wants them, anyone who will reach out a helpless hand and say, "I do want to change." Toward whom? "Toward those people in my life who do not deserve to be treated this way."

And that is why we do not want it. There is a price on our love. We want to be treated gently. We will exchange gentleness for a certain level of conduct. It is interesting that when you pinpoint the fact that a person does not want to give up being upset, he will get angry with you. He would rather have his own way. The sweetest music to anybody's ears is, "Do it my way. I think so clearly." The Bible says:

> **All we like sheep have gone astray;**
> **We have turned, every one, to his own way;**
> **And the Lord has laid on Him the iniquity of us all.**
>
> ISA. 53:6

Time and time again I enter into a struggle with men and women over whether or not God can give them peace in their circumstances. I do not understand why people struggle with this, and neither do I understand why they cease to struggle. But sooner or later, some will repent. How did the young man turn out? He eventually did repent. It is a mystery to me. He was able to love the same wife that he resented, and she did not change a bit. He did.

DEALING WITH THE INVISIBLE

The Pastor's Heart

Pastor, I want to give you an opportunity to look at some of the invisible sides of life. Even though they are invisible, they are very real. You have never seen resentment, but you have felt it. You cannot see deceit, but it is common.

> But if you have bitter envy and self-seeking in your hearts, do not boast and lie against the truth. This wisdom does not descend from above, but is earthly, sensual, demonic. For where envy and self-seeking exist, confusion and every evil thing are there.
>
> JAMES 3:14–16

Bitter envying and selfish ambition in the heart does not show. You can be very hostile toward a man, and walk up to him and put your arm around him and say, "Hi, friend." You can hide the inner thought of your soul by developing your acting ability. If you practice looking like a Christian, you will look a lot more like one a year from now than you do now. But your spirit may not have changed. The Christian life does not depend on your ability to act right but to "be" right. You may kid the world, but you will not fool yourself or God.

You have never seen resentment, but you have felt it. You cannot see deceit, but it is common.

You can have envying and selfish ambition in your heart, and nobody will know the difference. When you treasure these destructive things in your heart, physicians tell you that you will ache somewhere. You have abdominal aches and pains. You go to your physician, and he may tell you that there is no physiological problem. Some people are nervous, but there is nothing wrong with their nerves.

Here is a message that is potent, effective, and necessary, anywhere in the world. You hear people talking about their physical complaints. What we want is something we can swallow, something we can do to find relief.

Along with a spirit of disagreement and antagonism and bitterness, you will find confusion. People want to believe something about themselves that is not true. It is surprising how confused intelligent people can be.

Your heart—this invisible side of you—is part of your image that you need to keep polished, this invisible side of you. Love, peace, gentleness, longsuffering—all these are invisible, but they are there. On the other hand, I cannot see strife, envy, bitterness, or stubbornness, but they are real, too.

> *No human being or circumstances can interfere with your being filled with the Spirit.*

Are you still clinging to the flesh? Do you enjoy it? Even now, you are not sure that you want to give it up. All I can do is tell you there is a power available from above. All you need to do is receive it. You hold the key. I am talking about the relationship between you and your God. And the wonder of this message is that if you turn toward God, through Jesus Christ, God's power is available to you. Your mother, or your father, or the people you work with, cannot interfere with this power. With whom will you place your heart? The choice is yours. Which way will you choose?

> **We are ambassadors for Christ, as though God were pleading through us: we implore you on Christ's behalf, be reconciled to God.**
>
> 2 COR. 5:20

Hope, joy, peace (Rom. 15:13), love, patience, kindness, goodness, faithfulness, gentleness, and self-control (Gal. 5:22–23) are available on demand directly from God if you meet His conditions.

No human being or circumstances can interfere with your being filled with the Spirit.

> **Now the works of the flesh are evident, which are: adultery, fornication, uncleanness, lewdness, idolatry, sorcery, hatred, contentions, jealousies, outbursts of wrath, selfish ambitions, dissensions, heresies, envy, murders, drunkenness, revelries, and the like.**
>
> GAL. 5:19–21

These are called acts of the sinful nature.

HELPING OTHERS EXAMINE THEMSELVES

Pastor, you or someone in your congregation may have a similar problem with these invisible annoyances. The following examples may help you.

One day the wife of a Christian young man left him. There had been strains in the marriage, but this move surprised him. He was depressed—he lost interest in his business, had trouble sleeping, didn't care what or where he ate. He was bitter toward his wife, but he told me that his first concern was to do God's will.

> **And whatever you do, do it heartily, as to the Lord and not to men.**
>
> COL. 3:23

It is God's will that we go to Him for peace and comfort in all our tribulations. Yet this young man was letting his business run down. It was hard to find comfort and peace in his circumstances. Yes, his wife had left him. But wouldn't God give him comfort and peace under such circumstances? Was that too hard for God?

This man spoke in general terms of surrendering his life to God, but he failed to bring the details and circumstances of his life to God. In a sense, he was dissatisfied with what God had allowed and did not want to be happy. He insisted that his marital problem caused his bitterness. He refused to see that his marital problem was between him and his wife, and his bitterness involved him and God.

People tell me over and over again that some of the most miserable people they know are Christians. Why? Because many Christians do not face themselves as they are and take their problems to God. They make adjustments apart from God that will make them comfortable. It is like living with a sore thumb. The first day you will hit it a few times. You will soon learn to keep it out of the way. People have, so to speak, sore thumbs. If they avoid certain people or circumstances and refuse to get involved in certain conversations, they will keep themselves comfortable and free of pain.

You may have too much pressure at your job or as pastor of a church. Get a church or job with less pressure, and you will be OK. This may actually be effective—for awhile. If you get out from under these circumstances your condition will not be evident. It will be there, but it will be dormant. If the reason for the pressure was rebellion, the pressure will return when you are asked to do something you don't want to do. Relief from rebellion can come by changing jobs, but a cure for rebellion is to turn to God to cleanse your heart.

A young woman had habits that disturbed her mother. Both were Christians. The mother kept insisting that her misery was caused by her daughter's behavior. Accordingly, the mother felt quite clear in her own mind that the solution to her problem was to change her daughter. Further, this woman believed that she could not be agreeable toward her daughter lest she seem to be giving her blessing upon her daughter's unacceptable habits. She thought she was being a good Christian mother by being angry and impatient with her daughter. This woman did not even want peace.

This mother's main problem was her inner reaction to her daughter. Once she got her own attitudes straightened out, then and only then would she be ready to deal with her daughter's actions. The daughter needed correction because her behavior did not conform to God's Word. There were two separate circumstances here.

Which should this woman have worked on first? Herself.

I as a counselor should help you to see yourself as you are for your sake. I should not help you because it will make me happy. If I were to depend on the company I keep for my happiness and joy, I would be one of the most miserable people of all!

One day I had thirteen appointments. A thirteen-hour-long recital of problems and ills, yet I enjoyed it. My joy does not come from what I listen to; my joy comes from God. So congenial companions or a wonderful environment are not necessary for you to be joyful. The joy of the Lord is the fruit of His Spirit. His Spirit will give you joy no matter what is happening around you.

To help others examine themselves in the light of the Bible is what I call *evaluation*. Pastor, you may have many people to evaluate, but do not forget your own heart. To accept yourself as the Bible describes you is hard to do. It is so easy to quote the verse,

If we confess our sins, He is faithful and just to forgive us our sins and to cleanse us from all unrighteousness.

1 JOHN 1:9

I find that people shrink away from this kind of confession. It is much easier for us to correct our outward behavior. Jesus warned,

> **Then the Lord said to him, "Now you Pharisees make the outside of the cup and dish clean, but your inward part is full of greed and wickedness. Foolish ones! Did not He who made the outside make the inside also?"**
>
> LUKE 11:39–40

So our behavior, our thoughts, feelings, desires, actions, speech, must be identified in detail and dealt with separately.

People become morbidly introspective when they examine their "inward parts." They wear a "how sad I am" kind of look. Doesn't that prove their sincerity? Many people insist that a period of depression, self-condemnation, sadness, remorse, or weeping is evidence of repentance. I encounter people who are very sorry because they got caught. But that is not repentance. The Bible tells us quite clearly:

> **He who covers his sins will not prosper, But whoever confesses and forsakes them will have mercy.**
>
> PROV. 28:13

We must accept our behavior for what it is and confess it to God. Then that behavior needs to be forsaken. We must admit to God, "Yes, I am that way. No excuses, no alibis. I am that way, and I am sorry." People who approach God on this basis will find the peace and joy available only from God.

Wanted—Ambassadors for Christ. Your market is the church and the world. But first make sure you deal with your own sin, and then your message will be clear as you help God's people to do the same!

─────────── **HENRY T. BLACKABY** ───────────

THE REALITY OF SIN

Pastors must deal with the awful reality of sin—sin in their own life, sin in the people of God, and sin in the multitude of lost people around them. No life or ministry can know victory, success, and joy that ignores the reality of sin and God's solution and provision for sin.

God calls His pastors and His people to this incredible "ministry of reconciliation" as though God Himself were doing it through them (2 Cor. 5:18–19). All the fullness of God dwells in His shepherd and His people! All God's great salvation is in the hands of His people. God's Good News to a broken world has been given to His people to proclaim freely to all people. And God Himself is present to implement all of it in the lives of any who believe and obey Him.

But sin is always at work in this process:

> *No life or ministry can know victory, success, and joy that ignores the reality of sin and God's solution and provision for sin.*

But where sin abounded, grace abounded much more.

ROM. 5:20

What is impossible to men is possible with God (Matt. 19:26). And to the trusting servant of God with faith as a mustard seed, nothing will be impossible to him (Matt. 17:20).

In our hurting world there is no substitute for God's provisions. Therefore it is mandatory that pastors courageously share God's Word, faithfully, with great confidence—for God is present in such sharing to make every truth effective in the life of the one who hears and believes and obeys Him.

I once spoke from God's Word at Glorieta Conference Center in New Mexico. The next day a pastor approached me and said,

> Henry, you did not know this, but I came here determined and convinced to go back home to my church and resign next Sunday. As you spoke, God clearly spoke to my life through the Scripture message and told me I was the problem. It was not my people or my circumstances that I had been blaming, it was me! God clearly showed me my sin and what I must do. I obeyed the Lord, and now I have incredible joy and freedom from my sin. I'm going back and asking forgiveness from my people for not being the pastor

they have wanted and needed. I will covenant with them to be a new pastor for them by God's grace!

We prayed together and rejoiced together in what God had done with sin in his life! The pastor had been avoiding God's provision and had been turning to books, human reasoning, feelings, and anger. Lovingly and faithfully sharing God's Word had confronted him with truth, and this truth had set him free (John 8:31–32, 36). I see this happening constantly. I see this in lay people, in youth and college students, and in young, median, and senior adults. I see this in professional people and in laboring people.

THE WORLD'S ANSWER—DENIAL

However, many pastors are allowing themselves to be influenced by the philosophy of the world, sometimes presented convincingly by friends or by well-meaning Christian writers or counselors. When a pastor is persuaded by sociologists and human reasoning that the world and its logic will work, his ministry will be full of stress and failure. Sociologists and psychologists who do not have *sin* in their vocabulary do not treat sin as the problem; therefore they have no capacity to cure. Only God has made full provision for sin. Since the root of most problems is sin, the pastor must deal with sin.

When a pastor is persuaded by sociologists and human reasoning that the world and its logic will work, his ministry will be full of stress and failure.

A number of couples representing several churches decided to gather together one night each week to work through *The Heart of the Problem* study. During the first session the leader made the statement, "If sin is your problem, there is no human remedy." A certain young lady, Meg, became very upset and made a decision not to come back to the study. Her complaint to her husband was, "Sin is not my problem." Her husband encouraged her not to return to the study.

After all, she was a victim: she had been sinned against as a child. Meg had been sexually abused repeatedly when she was a child by many family members; she was a victim of incest. She could not understand how anyone could be so cold and uncaring as to even insinuate that sin would be *her* problem. She had been seeing a psychiatrist for seven years and was on medication that kept her asleep most of the time. The other couples stayed in the group.

Upon completing this study, one of the ladies decided to begin a group with some of the ladies in her church. Meg enrolled in this same study a second time. This time she stayed. When the group reached the chapter on forgiveness, Meg read the testimony titled, "I Want to Forgive Those Soldiers." God showed her that she was an angry, resentful, bitter, and unforgiving person. Meg's heart began to break. She asked God to forgive her, to cleanse her, and to fill her with His love, joy, peace, and forgiveness.

Her psychiatrist was one of the first to ask, "What happened to you? You look different!" She truly did look different. So different that when the leader of the initial *Heart of the Problem* group saw her at a reunion fellowship, he had to ask, "Who is that lady?" He was surprised to find out it was Meg.

A few days after Meg's change of heart, she began to experience spells of blacking out. She contacted her psychiatrist. The only explanation found was that Meg's body was rejecting the medications that she had been taking for years. The psychiatrist began immediately to wean her from all medications. Meg had turned to a source of help for seven years only to be left with all of the fruit of sin manifest in her life. God made her whole immediately.

God's Answer—Wholeness

Pastor, you are primarily dealing with sin as Jesus was. Jesus' message in His day was: "Repent! For the kingdom of heaven is near you!" This was His call:

1. Turn from your sin—it is destroying you.
2. Turn to heaven's full provision for your sin. The Kingdom of Heaven is right next to you.
3. Trust God to cleanse you and make you whole.

All through Jesus' ministry, people who believed Him, who trusted Him enough to call on Him to heal them, were made whole immediately. One woman was typical, not only of her day but ours:

> Now a certain woman had a flow of blood for twelve years,
> and had suffered many things from many physicians. She had
> spent all that she had and was no better, but rather grew
> worse.
>
> MARK 5:25–26

GOD'S SUFFICIENCY IN DEALING WITH SIN

Jesus never "made referrals" to anyone else. He and His Father
were present to bring all the help they needed. In my ministry as a
pastor for almost thirty years I never made referrals when sin was the
problem. God's resources were available, sufficient, and powerfully
effective. I never "referred someone to the world" where I knew God
could provide. Psalm 50:15 is very real to me:

> "Call upon Me in the day of trouble;
> I will deliver you, and you shall glorify Me."

How much honor has been denied our Lord when we make referrals
to the world and do not call on Him?

A lady once asked, "How do you know when a person needs 'big time'
help?" She was asking how to know when to refer a person to someone
greater than God! How much more "big time" can you get than God?

The world not only is unable to deal with sin, it does not even
acknowledge the reality of sin. You, pastor, are God's personal repre-
sentative for and with Him in your world to help people deal with sin.
Sin is the root cause of most personal problems, of most marital and
family problems—yes, even of most church problems.

Pastor, you are, or need to be, or must become, an expert in dealing
with sin! Jesus gave the disciples their assignment in these words:

> "And that repentance and remission of sins should be
> preached in His name to all nations, beginning at Jerusalem."
>
> LUKE 24:47

> "And you are witnesses of these things."
>
> LUKE 24:48

> "But tarry in the city of Jerusalem until you are endued with
> power from on high."
>
> LUKE 24:49

I never shared with others that I was an expert in anything else, in helping people deal with their sin. That was my call from God, and He has been enabling me to do it for years. I was

"not disobedient to the heavenly vision"

ACTS 26:19

I have witnessed God's setting people and families and churches free almost daily—and do so to this very hour.

Pastor, rethink from God's perspective your role in helping people be free from the bondage of their sin. Reestablish in your heart and ministry this crucial factor of sin from this point of view. Only you and God's people have this calling. Do it confidently! Do it courageously! Do it thoroughly! Do it to bring honor and glory to God, who will set people free by His power, through you and your church, to the utter amazement of a watching world.

PROCESS THE MESSAGE

1. Have you found yourself dealing with sin in a person's life simply by trying to correct the circumstances?

2. Did God deal with you about any particular sin in your life as you read this chapter? Have you repented?

3. Why is the pastor the best equipped person in the community to help people deal with sin?

4. Have you shied away from dealing with sin because you thought you did not have enough training? If so, why is that wrong thinking?

5. What change will take place in your life as a result of reading the message from the Scriptures in this chapter?

FIVE

Redemptive Preaching

My speech and my preaching were not with persuasive words of human wisdom, but in demonstration of the Spirit and of power, that your faith should not be in the wisdom of men but in the power of God.
1 CORINTHIANS 2:4–5

The preacher should not evaluate the effect of a sermon by the people who come forward in response to an invitation or by the people who tell him it was helpful.
HENRY BRANDT

Pastor, preach with a view to providing God's answers to people needs and expect God to interact with His people to bring them to fullness of life.
HENRY T. BLACKABY

HENRY BRANDT

I propose that the minister sees himself as a shepherd. First, let's attempt to define *shepherding:*

> *Shepherding*—A process between the minister and one or more persons by which the minister draws upon his biblical knowledge and his personal relationship with God to improve the spiritual health of one or more persons by means of preaching, teaching, or redemptive conversations.

We need to remind ourselves of the nature of our primary tool—the Bible.

> **For the word of God is living and powerful, and sharper than any two-edged sword, piercing even to the division of soul and spirit, and of joints and marrow, and is a discerner of the thoughts and intents of the heart.**
>
> HEB. 4:12

> **Your word I have hidden in my heart,**
> **That I might not sin against You.**
>
> PS. 119:11

POWER OF THE MESSAGE

Redemptive preaching should cause each person on his own to examine himself and to locate himself, spiritually speaking.

Redemptive preaching should cause each person on his own to examine himself and to locate himself, spiritually speaking. The pastor of a church where I spoke took us to a dinner meeting in the beautiful home of a builder. Until recently the builder would do anything he needed to do to make a buck. He drove his daughter to Sunday school on Sunday mornings and then would return to work on his buildings. As time went by, it became too inconvenient for him to drive home and return to pick her up. There was a church service the same time as Sunday school. In order to save himself a trip, he slipped into the back pew just to wait for his daughter. Over a period of three or four weeks the message from the pulpit pierced his heart. Now he spends his Sundays in worship and rest.

There is something miraculous about preaching. Preaching is cooperating with God, and the mystery of it all is that God can use an ordinary person to communicate His message to His people. This is redemptive preaching. This is a tremendous tool for you to use.

I visited a Bible college and there met Mr. Baird. He had a very influential, high-paying job. Mr. Baird was visiting a client and went to hear his minister one Sunday morning. The message caused Mr. Baird to examine himself. He realized that he was a self-centered, dishonest man. How did that realization come? Through the power of the message. Today Mr. Baird is the business manager of a Bible school. That sermon was the beginning of a new life for that man. This is redemptive preaching.

One reason that I am writing today is because of the power of preaching. Years ago I heard a missionary—John VanderSchie. I was a self-centered, hard-driving engineer. Yet that man's burden for people moved my heart. I wanted to meet him. I showed him my engineering department, my new home, my new car, and I took him out sailing in my boat. I wanted to impress him with things I had accumulated.

Little did I realize that when I took him on my sailboat, I was trapped. He began pouring out his burden for people. The combination of that man's message and my personal contact with him caused me to realize that all I was interested in was my material possessions.

John's goal was to cause me to consider my ways, such as how I conceived my job; what I did with my money; and what I did with my property. What difference did it make to the work of the church that I made good investments? What did I do with my time? How did I treat my wife? What did I do as a dad? How did I carry out my responsibilities in the church? John caused me to consider all these questions. John's purpose toward me was redemptive.

This verse describes the character and spirit a minister ought to have toward his audience:

> **Now I myself am confident concerning you, my brethren, that you also are full of goodness, filled with all knowledge, able also to admonish one another.**
>
> ROM. 15:14

Such a pastor will preach and teach the message that has warmed his heart without fear of offending people. If you plan your sermons in such a way that they do not step on anybody's toes, you will not be very effective. If there is something in a person's life that makes listening to your message difficult, your response ought to be that you are available to help them discover and correct any flaws in their lives.

Freedom from Fear

I talk to leaders who are afraid of people. Why? Let me call attention to a verse that points out one reason:

> **There is no fear in love; but perfect love casts out fear, because fear involves torment. But he who fears has not been made perfect in love.**
>
> 1 JOHN 4:18

What does that mean? It means that if a person is afraid, one question that he must face is whether his love toward someone is imperfect. Who irritates you?

A person who loves people with God's love is fearless. Often people have talked to me about their fears. I would ask them to tell me about their relationship to people. Who irritates you? They look at me and say, "How do you know?" How do I know? I have faith in God and His Word and its analysis of fear and its effect.

If you are afraid, pay attention to your relationships and your reactions to people. The more I think about this subject of redemptive preaching and teaching, the more I realize that what we are talking about is the *character* of the preacher. A man who loves his people will find a way to get his message across.

If a minister stands up in the pulpit in fear and trembling, wondering what the people will think of him, he cannot give himself to the audience. Obviously, if you are to have a redemptive relationship to your people, you need to have their attention.

One Sunday I was faced with a very sleepy, disinterested audience. It is not egotism to have a message burning on your heart that you believe God gave you and you think it will be of help to everyone. You would not want anyone to miss it. I think it is important and necessary that you have that kind of conviction about the message God gives you to share.

FINDING COMMON GROUND

I have discovered that a true story will get the attention of an audience. There is a biblical principle involved:

> **No temptation has overtaken you except such as is common to man.**
>
> 1 COR. 10:13

So I started out my sermon with a true story: In my senior year of college we were preparing to have the president of the college over for supper. You should have seen the preparations we made. That house was cleaner than it had ever been before. We were all uncomfortable in it. We were supposed to act like it was always that way. We told our three little children what they should say and what they could not say. We practically wrote them a script. (Preschool children do not follow scripts.)

As we sat around the dinner table, we were absorbed listening to what the scholarly man had to say. Sue, the smallest child, was sitting next to him. (That was another mistake.)

She asked him, "Would you pass the salt?" Nobody paid any attention to her little bitty voice. She asked him again. It did not work.

She pulled him by the sleeve and said, "Will you pass the salt or I will knock your block off."

I have told that story all around the world, and everybody thinks it is funny. What puzzles me is why I did not think it was funny. I was so mad at that little child. Yet really all she did was expose me. She did not cause anything; she revealed something.

It would be wonderful if we could enjoy going through situations like that as much as we enjoy reminiscing about them. This is the essence of the Christian life—to enjoy what you are doing.

Now that I had their attention I could proceed with an application. Compare my response to my daughter with this plumb line:

> **Be kindly affectionate to one another with brotherly love, in honor giving preference to one another.**
>
> ROM. 12:10

The college president was coming. My wife and I wanted to be at our very best. But our preparation was relating to the environment. I was so preoccupied in getting ready to look good for the president that I was not paying attention to my own inner life. An innocent little child exposed the whole thing. One of the benefits of being married and having children is that you can keep up to date on your spiritual life by paying attention to your response to what is happening. These unexpected little twists and turns in the road give you a glimpse of yourself—what you do about those glimpses is very important to you.

Combining a biblical principle with a true story is effective, yet you must handle a true story carefully. Can some detail be left out that would protect the subject's identity? It is best to request permission from the subject of the story.

I often give a series of messages over a period of three to five days. Frequently I will see a counselee during the day and listen to a story that is almost word for word like an illustration I plan to use that night. I have planned the sermon weeks ago. To use it that night might seem like a betrayal of the counselee's confidence; therefore I will usually choose a different illustration.

I was a visiting speaker at a church one evening. My sermon was about letting the Lord remove bitterness, wrath, and anger from the heart. The pastor told me that he came to the meeting with an ongoing problem on his mind involving the church. My sermon gave him the answer. He was afraid to tackle the problem because he was irritated with the people involved. He did not love them. He was angry at them. He had convinced himself that he could be irritated and love them at the same time.

Anger is a work of the flesh. Love is a fruit of the Spirit. They do not coexist. What he needed to do first of all was take care of personal sins (anger and resentment) and replace them with God's love. Then he could deal with the church problem without fear. That is redemptive preaching.

Ministers spread a biblical principle across the audience, trusting it will seek out those who need it. You can reach a thousand people with a biblical principle just as easily as sharing it with one person in your study. By the way, that pastor was in the audience one day when I told his story. I used his story with his permission.

Let's look again at my illustration about the minister. You do not know who I was talking about, but you can think of people who are like him. All temptation is common. Anything you say by illustration is common if it describes human behavior. If you want to speak to everyone in the audience, make sure your illustration happened to someone. The details may vary, but there are boundaries to the works of the flesh and the fruit of the Spirit. In your mind you may be describing one person. People in your audience will have someone else in mind. Strip this minister of his title and you have anyone who was angrily pouting because he could not have his way. How many children, wives, husbands, employees, men, and women in your audience are experiencing the same problem?

This is an important point: Personal experiences can become information that everyone can identify with—a basis for redemptive preaching.

The Power of God's Spoken Word

I was reluctantly drawn to the speaking platform by people whom I was able to help in the consulting room. I had accepted the notion that the pulpit was no longer an effective way to help people redemptively. The pastor's study is the place. This is what I was taught.

What would I talk about? In the consulting room I listened to the stories people told me in relation to a plumb line, the Bible. I listened with a compassionate, loving heart. My diagnosis was helpful only if the counselee was ready to face the truth and act on it.

After several years of listening in the consulting room it began to dawn on me that the stories people tell me repeat themselves. The details vary, but the underlying drive is a work of the flesh. The solutions also became repetitive because human behavior is repetitive. I decided to share on the platform what I learned while talking with people.

One Sunday a lady I had never met came up to me. She said, "I want you to know that I was in one of your audiences in January, and you said some things about child-parent relationships that really helped me. I came to that meeting very burdened because I did not know what to do with my teenage daughter. In the four months since then, my husband and I have brought order into our home."

That is one simple illustration of the fact that people are capable of picking up truths from your sermons and making application in their own lives. What do you say when people ask, "That sermon, did you mean it for me?" My answer would be, "Why, certainly, I meant it for you. Which part of it applies?"

I learned something recently while listening to a sermon given on TV. When the pastor finished, I changed channels and there he was on another station beginning his sermon. I listened to it again and received an entirely different message from the same sermon.

The preacher should not evaluate the effect of a sermon by the people who come forward in response to an invitation or by the people who tell him it was helpful. You may never know who the Lord will touch through your sermons. As an example, this is an excerpt of a letter sent to a friend of mine:

> I've been thinking a lot about the weekend we spent with you when Dr. Henry Brandt spoke at your church. . . . The Sunday I sat and listened to his message, I was close to becoming a "basketcase." And to whom does a missionary on furlough go to explain such a thing? The few people I had tried to communicate with either thought I was neurotic or started telling me their own problems. I talked to our pastor and got the feeling he did not feel capable of counseling me. He recommended a Christian counselor who charged $75.00 for each 45-minute session (which, as you know, is a fortune to a missionary).
>
> I had explained at the onset that there was stress in my life I couldn't change, and I needed to learn how to deal with it. Brandt had all these nice little charts he hauled out at each session. I kept waiting for him to get through the introduction and help me personally. What happened is that after going through all his charts, I explained what I had said at the onset, that I know these things in my mind, but how do I control the emotional roller coaster I was on?
>
> So he gave me the zinger—if it wasn't working for me, there must be hidden sin in my life! That's just what you need to tell a person who is honestly seeking help—that it is all their fault! Anyway, all I know is that sitting in that meeting in your church, listening to Dr. Brandt was some sort of turning point for me. All he said was such common sense and just what I needed. What I didn't know at the time was that years ago he spent months here ministering to missionaries. One of the missionaries who founded the hospital here shared some really neat stories of the time Dr. Brandt was here. I wish I could be more specific. But, as I said, it is hard to put on paper emotional struggles.
>
> Now that I look back on those two very difficult years, it is frightening when I see how wrong so many of my attitudes were. I had formed some very negative attitudes and responses to those closest to me. We were all suffering

deeply because of our daughter's problems. The emotional swings she was going through and the emotional swings I was going through with the beginning of menopause were like a match to paper. Yet it is hard to explain the way I felt. I truly felt that everyone was against me. I felt hurt, wounded, betrayed—feeling the classic victim and not even realizing it. I think the thing I like best about Dr. Brandt is his forthright manner. He says it like it is.

You may never know how helpful your sermon can be.

Do Not Neglect Your Heart

One of the great mysteries to me is that God can minister through His Word even though the preacher delivers it with a cold, deceitful heart.

I have observed a strange plague spreading across the land. Too many ministers are falling by the wayside in spite of the fact they have an effective ministry. People are accepting the Lord; Christians are benefiting from an inspiring pulpit ministry; the church staff is productive. Out of the blue comes the chilling announcement that the pastor has misused some money, or has become emotionally involved with one or more women, or he is drinking, or divorcing. How is this possible?

I hear the same dreary reason. The use of the Bible continues long after the pastor's heart has grown cold because of unresolved conflicts in or out of the church. The Bible describes this condition:

> **For as he thinks in his heart, so is he. "Eat and drink!" he says to you, But his heart is not with you.**
>
> **PROV. 23:7**

He keeps up the appearance and continues serving God's precious, powerful words. He does not know it, but he is modeling the truth of God's words.

> **"For as the rain comes down, and the snow from heaven,**
> **And do not return there,**
> **But water the earth,**
> **And make it bring forth and bud,**

> That it may give seed to the sower
> And bread to the eater,
> So shall My word be that goes forth from My mouth;
> It shall not return to Me void,
> But it shall accomplish what I please,
> And it shall prosper in the thing for which I sent it.
>
> Isa. 55:10–11

He is relieved because the people are responding to his sermons. He would be advised to pay attention to a simple little warning:

> **Therefore let him who thinks he stands take heed lest he fall.**
>
> 1 Cor. 10:12

Read the entire chapter later.
Do not neglect your heart!

------------   **HENRY T. BLACKABY**   ------------

PREACH FROM A CLEAN HEART

Indeed, you must not neglect your heart. Preaching and teaching must proceed from a heart that is clean before the Lord. The truth of the Word will be present whether your heart is right or not. However, God gives no room for your heart to be wrong when preaching His message to His people. If it is wrong, you will know immediately because the condition of your heart contradicts your message, and the Spirit of God will convict you!

Eliphaz found this out the hard way. His counsel to Job had not been right. It had not been from the Lord. God had confronted Job, and Job cried out:

> *You asked,* "Who *is* this who hides counsel without knowledge?"
> Therefore I have uttered what I did not understand,
> Things too wonderful for me, which I did not know. . . .
> I have heard of You by the hearing of the ear,
> But now my eye sees You.
> Therefore I abhor myself,
> And repent in dust and ashes.
>
> Job 42:3, 5–6

God then confronted Eliphaz and said,

> **My wrath is aroused against you and your two friends, for you have not spoken of Me what is right, as My Servant Job has. Now therefore, take for yourselves seven bulls and seven rams, go to My servant Job, and offer up for yourselves a burnt offering; and My servant Job shall pray for you. For I will accept him, lest I deal with you according to your folly.**
>
> JOB 42:7–8

Anyone who shares God's Word with God's people must have a clean heart in God's sight. The Bible describes Jesus' ministry as consisting of teaching, preaching, and *healing*. Lives were constantly being changed when people were around Jesus. Within His message was the presence and power of God to bring healing and wholeness to others.

> **And they were astonished at His teaching, for He taught them as one having authority, and not as the scribes.**
>
> MARK 1:22

> **Jesus answered and said to him, "If anyone loves Me, he will keep My word; and My Father will love him, and We will come to him and make Our home with him.**
>
> JOHN 14:23

The pastor has the same Word of God. He can and should preach and teach with confident assurance that the One who sent him, and gave him a message, will be present to implement the Truth in the life of anyone who hears and obeys.

Jesus said that whoever comes to Him, hears His Word, and obeys

> **is like a man building a house, who dug deep and laid the foundation on the rock. And when the flood arose, the stream beat vehemently against that house, and could not shake it, for it was founded on the rock.**
>
> LUKE 6:48

PREACH WITH EXPECTANCY

Preaching creates the occasion for God's people, in worship, to come to Him, hear His Word, and obey Him. If the people respond, their lives will be deeply affected. It is therefore crucial that the Word they hear comes faithfully through a devoted servant of God.

No one else can give such assurance to people as the pastor who faithfully preaches God's message. God gives the pastor a message, because

- God knows who is going to be present to hear it;
- God will be present to enable the pastor to courageously and lovingly share it; and
- God will be there working in the hearts of the hearers causing them to understand it and want to respond to it.

Paul confirms this:

> **It pleased God through the foolishness of the message preached to save those who believe.**
>
> 1 COR. 1:21

Paul was so convinced of the present and active power of God when he preached that he said,

> **My speech and my preaching were not with persuasive words of human wisdom, but in demonstration of the Spirit and of power, that your faith should not be in the wisdom of men but in the power of God.**
>
> 1 COR. 2:4–5

The pastor must preach and teach with expectancy, believing that God will change lives!

After a message I had preached, a lady approached me and asked me to pray with her. She said she was going to see a lawyer the next day and proceed with a divorce. I knew God had been present in the service, so I asked her to let me read from Malachi 2:13–16.

> **And this is the second thing you do:**
> **You cover the altar of the LORD with tears,**
> **With weeping and crying;**
> **So He does not regard the offering anymore,**
> **Nor receive it with goodwill from your hands.**
> **Yet you say, "For what reason?"**

Because the L<small>ORD</small> has been witness
Between you and the wife of your youth,
With whom you have dealt treacherously;
Yet she is your companion
And your wife by covenant.
But did He not make them one,
Having a remnant of the Spirit?
And why one?
He seeks godly offspring.
Therefore take heed to your spirit,
And let none deal treacherously with the wife of his youth.
"For the L<small>ORD</small> God of Israel says That He hates divorce,
For it covers one's garment with violence,"
Says the L<small>ORD</small> of hosts.
"Therefore take heed to your spirit,
That you do not deal treacherously."

M<small>AL</small>. 2:13–16

She stopped and said, "No one ever told me that! I didn't know that! Will you pray for me because tomorrow I'm going to have my lawyer cancel the divorce proceedings. I will seek reconciliation with my husband!"

What incredible blessing God brings and effects in people's lives through a faithful preaching and teaching of God's Word. One message, faithfully delivered, can be used by the Holy Spirit to touch the brokenness and despair of many. God can heal the wounded, "free the captives," give light to those in darkness and guidance to those seeking His will and His way. All this in one message!

> *God can heal the wounded, "free the captives," give light to those in darkness and guidance to those seeking His will and His way. All this in one message!*

I was preaching in a morning service with expectation for God to be working deeply in the hearts of those present. I noticed a young girl of about ten or eleven years. She came weeping and knelt at the altar. I waited thinking others would be expectant too. No one came to her side, so I left the pulpit and knelt with her. I heard her weeping for the salvation of a friend of hers. Soon I joined in praying confidently for God to hear her prayer. The service ended, and she went away with expectant joy on her face.

I preached the evening message also. At the invitation I noticed this same precious girl returning to the front. This time, she was weeping and holding the hand of her friend for whom she had prayed that morning. Her friend was coming to put her faith and trust in Jesus. Oh the power in preaching to touch lives, change lives, and bring great news to people!

Pastor, preach with a view to providing God's answers to people's needs and expect God to interact with His people to bring them to fullness of life.

One Sunday evening I was preaching in my first pastorate. Suddenly, the door to the worship center opened noisily, and in came twenty-four teenagers from a recently formed gang called, "The Untouchables." I continued to preach my heart out, knowing God must have brought them though they probably were unaware of His drawing love in their lives.

The church welcomed them. They came back. Within six months of hearing God's Word, twenty-three of the twenty-four had become Christians. It changed not only their lives, but the low-rent housing area from which many had come. I became their pastor, and our church became their church.

PREACH GOD'S WORD

But a serious caution is in order here. Be slow to quote men. Share what God says! Do not tell humorous stories that do not lead them to the Savior. Do not merely "craft a sermon." Passionately expound God's Truth, open its fullest meaning, illustrate from common life, apply it to people's needs, and urge them to respond to Him. Share with the people that God is present to love them, redeem them, and provide for them. Do all this with confident expectation and hope!

Two Important Truths

1. *Do Not Receive the Grace of God in Vain (2 Cor. 6:1).* Enormous grace (God's unlimited provision made available to you and God's

people) is actively at work before, during, and after your preaching. Treat God's mighty provision as a sacred trust. His Word, accompanied by the Enabler, the Holy Spirit, will produce in the lives of the hearers that for which God sent it (Isa. 55:10–13). God must be honored just in the proclamation of His Word.

> *Tremble yourself, as you preach!*
> *Weep with pain, or joy, as you preach!*
> *Exhort, plead, encourage, as you preach!*

Let all who hear you be aware that you are entrusted with all the grace of God and have come expectantly to see God express His grace to them.

> **And God *is* able to make all grace abound toward you, that you, always having all sufficiency in all things, may have an abundance for every good work.**
>
> 2 COR. 9:8

2. *You are a worker together with God (2 Cor. 6:1).* God is present, and He must be highly honored in your preaching. May all who hear sense that God is saying to them: "This is My greatly loved son, hear him!" God is just as present with us, whom He has sent, as He was with His Son, Jesus.

In the heart of God, witnessed by all the Scriptures, this is also true:

> **How beautiful upon the mountains**
> **Are the feet of him who brings good news,**
> **Who proclaims peace,**
> **Who brings glad tidings of good things,**
> **Who proclaims salvation,**
> **Who says to Zion,**
> **"Your God reigns!"**
> **Your watchmen shall lift up their voices,**
> **With their voices they shall sing together;**
> **For they shall see eye to eye**
> **When the LORD brings back Zion.**
> **Break forth into joy, sing together,**
> **You waste places of Jerusalem!**
> **For the LORD has comforted His people,**

He has redeemed Jerusalem.
The LORD has made bare His holy arm
In the eyes of all the nations;
And all the ends of the earth shall see
The salvation of our God.

ISA. 52:7–10

P R O C E S S   T H E   M E S S A G E

1. How would you know if your preaching was in the "power of the Spirit" instead of with human ability of persuasive words?

2. Does any person or group in your congregation or staff intimidate you?

3. Do you find yourself treating those with wealth more carefully than the poor person?

4. Do you cater to certain age groups of people more than others? Why?

5. Is there any area of your life where you continue to use "pastoral manners," yet your heart has grown cold toward the people you are ministering to?

6. Do you judge your own preaching by the number of decisions you see during the invitation?

7. Are you satisfied with speaking God's Word even if no one compliments your message?

8. Would you say the last message you delivered was a "well-crafted sermon" or a word from God?

9. What are you doing to nurture your soul?

SIX

Redemptive Conversations

> *The Lord God has given Me*
> *The tongue of the learned,*
> *That I should know how to speak*
> *A word in season to him who is weary.*
> *He awakens Me morning by morning,*
> *He awakens My ear*
> *To hear as the learned.*
> ISAIAH 50:4
>
> *If your confidence in God is shaken, you need to face up to*
> *what you are doing wrong.*
> HENRY BRANDT
>
> *Pastor, when you speak with hurting people, Think*
> *Scripture and Share Scripture.*
> HENRY T. BLACKABY

HENRY BRANDT

People often walk around with pleasant smiles and look relaxed. If you speak with them you get the impression that all is well, though they struggle with heavy burdens. The Bible describes these people:

> **The words of his mouth were smoother than butter,**
> **But war was in his heart;**
> **His words were softer than oil,**
> **Yet they were drawn swords.**
>
> Ps. 55:21

I struggled with the problem of how to discern whether a person's outward behavior is an accurate picture of one's inner life. There are many books written on the subject, however a Bible verse settled the problem for me:

> **For what man knows the things of a man except the spirit of the man which is in him? Even so no one knows the things of God except the Spirit of God.**
>
> 1 COR. 2:11

I try my best to take everyone at their word unless there is a specific reason why their word is questionable. I cannot discern the condition of their inner life.

There are many people, Christian and non-Christians, who are struggling with a vile concoction of evil thoughts, ugly desires, or old grudges—deceitful relationships, memories of physical or verbal abuse, or having been physically or verbally abusive themselves. Anything described as the acts of the sinful nature may be part of their struggle. There may be a mixture of anger, resentment, hatred, and rebellion. The effort to contain this inner condition can cause painful muscular tension, can affect breathing, digestion, and sleeping. This person is hurting and must find some relief. Yet none of this inner condition has to show in outward behavior.

When you are in a church or conference setting, it may be difficult to discern if the person wants to just have a social conversation or a redemptive conversation. However, the minister must constantly be sensitive to the Holy Spirit so he can know when to treat the conversation as redemptive. If the person simply wants someone to listen, he or she may not be ready to hear the truth. The servant of the Lord must trust the Lord to direct his speaking and listening. You would not probe for personal information in the area of feelings, emotions, and thoughts if this were just a social call.

Remember my definition of shepherding? Redemptive conversations should be encountered according to this standard:

> A process between a minister and one or more persons by which the minister draws upon his biblical knowledge and his personal relationship with God to improve the spiritual health of one or more persons by means of preaching, teaching, or redemptive conversations.

The Scriptures put it this way:

> **The Lord GOD has given Me**
> **The tongue of the learned,**
> **That I should know how to speak**
> **A word in season to him who is weary.**
> **He awakens Me morning by morning,**
> **He awakens My ear**
> **To hear as the learned.**
>
> ISA. 50:4

How fortunate for those who are struggling to find a kind, compassionate, accepting listener who can assist them in pouring out what troubles them—to "get it off their chests." This process brings blessed relief.

THERAPEUTIC LISTENING OR REDEMPTIVE LISTENING?

Most of my teachers in graduate school were among the finest people I ever met. They tried sincerely to be compassionate, kind, gentle, and accepting of everyone. They accepted me with my notion that the Bible is my guidebook, and I believed in a Savior. They taught me to grant anyone else the right to choose their own course.

I learned that I could help hurting people find blessed relief by serving them as a good listener. I could help them to become comfortable with or without confronting their sins. I was taught we do not need God in this process. I was taught we have ample resources in this world to enable one person to help another get comfortable.

These fine teachers were humanists. They did not recognize a creator of the universe. They believed that we have evolved. We must save ourselves, they said. They were good, ungodly people.

The Bible says,

> **Blessed is the man**
> **Who walks not in the counsel of the ungodly,**
> **Nor stands in the path of sinners,**
> **Nor sits in the seat of the scornful,**
>
> PS. 1:1

The opposite of this verse says that ungodly people are not blessed.

It slowly dawned on me that I was the disciple of humanists, even though I kept studying my Bible. I was beginning to think like a humanist. It was much easier to help troubled people live with their sins than to confront them with their sins. Why not take the easy way? People liked my work and recommended me to others who needed help.

Jesus said,

> **I give you my own peace and my gift is nothing like the peace of the world.**
>
> JOHN 14:27, PHILLIPS

The peace of this world is not the same as the peace that Jesus gives. But it is hard to tell them apart. There are substitutes that are close to the real thing. Compassionate listening without bringing our sinfulness in the picture is one of them. But this person is no closer to God than when you started listening to his story. He may be relieved but not blessed.

The biblical message is that Jesus came to save us from our sins and to give us access to the Spirit of God. To withhold this information from a troubled person is cruelty. It is heartless to help a person live comfortably with his sins. If it is sin, there is no human remedy—only God can help. The troubled person needs to know how to approach God, what God offers us, and how to appropriate His help.

Humanists are fine people. But they declare that there is no deity that can help us.

There are two kinds of helpful listening: *therapeutic listening and redemptive listening.*

In therapeutic listening, a kind and compassionate therapist will assist a troubled person to pour out what is troublesome—to help the person "get it off his chest."

In redemptive listening, a kind compassionate listener will also help a troubled person pour out his troubles, using biblical knowledge to identify the nature of the content. If any of it is sinful, this person needs to enter into the presence of God for forgiveness, cleansing, and empowering. The goals of therapeutic listening are unrelated to redemptive listening.

LISTEN WITH THE HOLY SPIRIT AS YOUR GUIDE

Listening is an art. Consider these factors of a good listener.

A Good Listener Loves People

A good listener must be a loving, compassionate person. You must love the person enough to present him with God's truth regardless of what the truth suggests. When the rich young ruler came to Jesus and asked what he must do to inherit eternal life,

> **Then Jesus, looking at him, loved him, and said to him, "One thing you lack: Go your way, sell whatever you have and give to the poor, and you will have treasure in heaven; and come, take up the cross, and follow Me."**
>
> MARK 10:21

But you must not force God's solution on the person. Remember that he has the freedom of choice. He can reject or accept God's answer to his problems. Jesus gave the rich young ruler a choice:

> **But he was sad at this word, and went away sorrowful, for he had great possessions.**
>
> MARK 10:22

He rejected what he had heard.

Listen to the Problem

As a "specialist" in spiritual problems (problems of the spirit, the inner man), you will, with the guidance of the Holy Spirit, seek to discover the individual's attitudes and reactions toward people and circumstances. This may take three or four interviews—or more. The process cannot be hurried.

You need not probe endlessly into the counselee's past. No one can change what has gone before. The person's current behavior and attitude, which reflect his past, is what you should be concerned with. Listen for evidences of carnality, works of the flesh, sin. You know that the blood of Jesus Christ can wash away sin and that the fruit of the Spirit can replace the works of the flesh. You should have the same confidence in the benefits of your message as the surgeon has in the benefits of an operation.

Then as you gain experience in depending on the Holy Spirit in counseling, your interviewing ability will improve. Obviously your one-hundredth counseling interview will go smoother than your first.

Point the Counselee to a Solution

Be sure you correctly understand the person's situation and his attitudes and reactions toward it. Do not jump to a solution hurriedly before you are sure of the exact nature of the problem based on the information given. Help the counselee put the problem in his own words.

When you and the counselee agree on his problem and understand his attitudes and reactions, you can then use the Bible as a mirror so the individual can see himself reflected there. At this point you need to faithfully, gently, patiently, and lovingly declare the Word of God.

After all, doesn't the Bible give God's answers to people's basic problems and needs?

> *A pastor can get himself into some difficult corners because he has pledged to keep confidences.*

Some counselors do not feel they should suggest any solutions to their counselee's problems. They believe that the individual must struggle and grope till he finally finds and accepts his own solution. But isn't it true that the person has come to you because he wants help—not only in understanding his problem but in finding a solution to it? Why should you withhold God's answers to a person's problems when you know the answers? You should present the biblical solution—and then it is up to the counselee to accept it or reject it.

If the individual is not a Christian, this is the time to present the plan of salvation—God's offer of forgiveness of sin through faith in Christ as one's personal Savior. If the individual is a Christian, this is the time to teach him about walking in the Spirit. It is surprising how often Christians will gradually drift away from the Lord and accept their sinful condition as "normal."

The next step is up to the counselee. He may repent, or he may not. He may want to go away and think about it. Or he may go away quite upset. Or he may ask to return for more help on clarifying the problem and understanding its solution.

Listen without Promising Confidentiality

This item may surprise you: *I will not commit myself to keeping confidences.* A pastor can get himself into some difficult corners because he has pledged to keep confidences. A troubled person may share information that is harmful to himself or others. I look upon my counselee as a member of the body of Christ. Sometimes the interests of the body must be protected over and above the individual.

For example, one of my counselees decided to commit suicide. Her problem was whether to kill herself by poison or using a gun. This is not to be kept confidential.

Or suppose one of these scenarios was happening:

- A pastor knows that his organist and Christian education director, both married, are lovers.
- There is continued misuse of church funds by the treasurer.
- A pastor must publicly deal with a teenager for drinking when he knows that an official of the church is doing the same thing.
- Two teenagers are sleeping together.
- A deacon tells you he wants to divide the church.

The pastor's hands would be tied if he agreed to keep the information confidential.

Because human behavior is so common I have concluded that I will not agree to keep a conversation confidential when I have no idea what I will hear. The person will have to trust me. I am not known as a man who goes around spreading stories. If they do not trust me, they should not come to me. I believe that the only effective kind of relationship between two people must involve faith and trust. If you want to take the risk of talking to me, you will also have to face the risk of trusting me with the information. Redemptive relationships require faith and trust. The relationship of faith and trust between the man that is speaking and the people who are listening is fundamental.

In fifty years of counseling, I have not once divulged confidential information without the permission of the person involved.

Speak to the Body of Christ

It is important for people to understand that you will teach them how to discern what is righteous or unrighteous. *As the minister your first interest is for the church body and not the person.* I think we have gotten that emphasis all twisted. We break the church body up into little pieces, and everybody is a private lonely person in a church full of people.

You could not run a business that way. You could not play on an athletic team unless you are willing to give yourself to the team. When an individual comes to me he is a member of the body. Many times I have used someone's conversation as an illustration—only with that person's permission however. By changing a few details, the person is protected. Remember:

> **No temptation has overtaken you except such as is common to man; but God is faithful, who will not allow you to be tempted beyond what you are able, but with the temptation will also make the way of escape, that you may be able to bear it.**
>
> 1 COR. 10:13

It is a fallacy that you can go your way and do what you want and think the way you want and at the same time be a part of the body.

I have not found that people object to my judicious use of their problem as an illustration, because I prayerfully seek to help the rest of the body through the illustration. Well, you try it. Give it some thought. After all, if your goal is to prepare a message that does not apply to anyone, you will succeed. Messages should speak to the body of Christ, not just to the individual.

You cannot talk about the center of a basketball team without thinking of this person as someone who is interacting and interrelated with the rest of the team. When you take a job, you are part of a work force. It is a fallacy that you can go your way and do what you want and think the way you want and at the same time be a part of the body.

Locate the Problem

When you deal with an individual in a congregation, you must think of that person with reference to the whole body. An irritant in a church can disrupt the church.

> **And if one member suffers, all the members suffer with it; or if one member is honored, all the members rejoice with it. Now you are the body of Christ, and members individually.**
>
> 1 Cor. 12:26–27

I think that is what Jesus meant when He said,

> **If your right eye causes you to sin, pluck it out and cast it from you; for it is more profitable for you that one of your members perish, than for your whole body to be cast into hell.**
>
> Matt. 5:29

Do not let an offensive eye ruin your whole body. From a redemptive standpoint then, what I am trying to do is *locate you* in a body. If you pastor a church or are a member of the church, ask yourself, "Am I an irritant or an asset to the body?" I look upon anyone to whom I speak individually simply as a member of a body.

Personal Problems within the Body

A young couple came to me who were on the verge of splitting up because they were frustrated sexually. Earlier they could not wait to get married because there was a tremendous physical attraction between them. Now the house was not big enough for the two of them. These are the same two people! She could not stand for him to touch her. I discovered there were some conflicts. He would come home from work and throw himself on the couch. She insisted that he change his clothes first.

His reaction was, "Look, I have been throwing myself on the couch all my life and nobody complained. Now I am married, and I have to change my clothes. I am not going to do it."

He was asserting himself. "I demand my right to throw myself on the couch in my dirty clothes." Then she said he should take his shoes off on the landing. "Take my shoes off on the landing?"

He had some pretty high requirements for her too. He wanted her to dress a certain way. He did not like the way she flavored the gravy.

They had many complaints against each other. People in that condition are certainly not going to fall into each other's arms. How can you express affection toward somebody for whom you have no affection— someone toward whom you have anger in your heart?

My advice. Take your shoes off on the landing. Change your clothes. Relax your demands on how she dresses and eat her gravy. He did and things improved, just like I said. I did not mention God. I did not use the Bible. All I did was juggle the environment a little bit and things improved. I became a wonderful counselor. They are still happy because they have resolved their problems.

But there is one more thing that I had to tell these people. Even though their relationship is better, and I helped them become more comfortable, I also had to tell them why. Do you know what I did? I appealed to his *selfishness*. He wanted something strongly enough to compromise in other areas. To get what he wanted he had to appeal to her *selfishness*. She was getting her own way.

> *As a pastor your assignment from God is not to make people comfortable with their sin, but to help them diagnose and deal with their sin.*

I helped these people improve their relationship on the basis of *mutual selfishness*. The couple did not deal with their real problem. They had not located themselves in the marriage or personally. I warned them that the adjustment was temporary. Sooner or later they would come up with another conflict. They had yet to face up to the fact of their own self-centeredness. People can improve relationships by making concessions without giving God a thought. Without a change of heart it will be temporary. Without a change of heart this couple had learned to live with their sins.

As a pastor your assignment from God is not to make people comfortable with their sin, but to help them diagnose and deal with their sin.

Does Your Heart Condemn You?

Occasionally I talk to ministers about people in their congregations who have doubts about whether or not they are saved. They want to talk to me. Usually these people have read some good books on the subject. They have been to their pastor—maybe even gone to a famous pastor or evangelist. They use the Scriptures to try to reassure these people that if they did certain things, they are saved. If they were not convinced by ministers who know a lot more about the Scriptures than I, then what have I to contribute?

A precious Bible verse will help to clear up the problem:

> **Beloved, if our heart does not condemn us, we have confidence toward God. And whatever we ask we receive from Him, because we keep His commandments and do those things that are pleasing in His sight.**
>
> 1 JOHN 3:21–22

I ask them, "Isn't that a great Bible verse?"

They answer, "Yes, that is a great verse."

I ask, "What does it mean?"

They do not have a clue. I am not trying to embarrass them. I want to make sure that they understand a very important biblical principle.

When a person gives you an answer indicating they understand when they do not, they may not be lying to you. They are probably giving you an unthinking, preoccupied answer. If you do not ask them to explain, you may assume that they understand when they do not understand.

If you turn that verse around, it says,

> **You will have confidence toward God if your heart does not condemn you.**

In other words, if your confidence in God is shaken, you need to discover what you are doing wrong.

Invariably, the person wants to change the subject and say, "I came to you because I am not sure I am saved."

I say, "I know that is why you came. One of the reasons that you are not sure you are saved may be because your heart condemns you. You need to discover what you are doing that condemns you. Or perhaps what or who are you loving that condemns you. This calls for some heart searching." This is what I would call redemptive activity.

If your confidence in God is shaken there may be something wrong with you. I say that without reservation and without knowing anything about you. I say it by faith in the Bible.

SIN AND ITS REMEDY

A common problem that plagues people is the struggle with a temper. Many people say they know they have a temper but can control it most of the time. But they say that they have a delicate disposition. They must be treated very gently. You see, they get upset if they are crossed.

A temper is not just a problem; a temper is sinful. The first step in cleansing is to acknowledge your sins. The next step is to repent. To admit to a temper is not repentance. People may admit their sin and be sorry, and want to do penance. Do something. Correct something. People cry, wring their hands, pace the floor, and say, "I must do something to make up for my sins."

You cannot do it. You must receive forgiveness. You reach out a helpless hand. What is wrong if you do not feel forgiven? Forgiveness is freely given to repentant people. It is not a complicated problem. The concept of receiving forgiveness is not hard to grasp. There is probably a reason why you do not feel forgiven, so let us investigate and find out what it is.

You need to be cleansed. I recall a person who asked to be forgiven for long-standing hatred, but did not want to give up the hatred. Yet being cleansed is not going far enough. You need to walk in the Spirit. One woman concluded now that she is forgiven and free, she will never let it happen again. She is depending on her willpower and determination.

One man said he had trouble with pornographic pictures. What was his solution? When he came to a theater, he crossed over to the other side of the street.

I said, "So you think dealing with your desire is a matter of eyesight? One of these days you will get trapped. You have not dealt with your problem."

He is trying to help himself. One of the most resisted ideas in the Bible is that we are weak, subject to temptation, and always will be. You may be inclined to spring to this man's defense. He is really a nice, sincere man. Only when we realize that God enables us to walk in the Spirit, will His power sustain us.

Your goal in redemptive conversations is to bring people to repentance! Unless people reach out with helpless hands to receive forgiveness for sin, and receive cleansing, and God's power and blessing, people will have their sinful self back again—it will always be available. People are free to be as difficult or as loving as they want. God will love people either way.

What Is Going On Beneath the Skin?

A lady came to the consulting room with this story: When her husband left that morning, he said he was coming home for lunch at 12:00. She liked that idea and decided to make him a nice lunch. She set a lovely table with nice dishes and a nice tablecloth. It got close to noon. She took a bath, combed her hair, and put on her makeup, fine perfume, and a nice dress.

Only one detail went wrong. He did not come. Five after, he was not there. Ten after, he was not there. This nice lady started getting angry. She was becoming madder and madder as the soup got colder and colder. Then the phone rang. It was her husband. He said he had been delayed but he was coming right over—with a friend.

In the meantime, she microwaved the soup and put another setting on the table. Once they arrived, the visitor said he did not care for any soup. She was really angry now. Her husband took one spoonful of the overheated soup and said, "Oh, why did you make it so hot?"

He said to his friend, "Come on, let's go." Away they went, leaving this fuming, sputtering woman behind. She was furious even though she was all alone. Let me ask you, have you taken sides?

I said to her, "You do not have to be upset."

She turned all her fury on me and said, disdainfully, "I suppose you think I should be happy!"

What an obnoxious idea to be happy! Imagine an individual fuming and spouting and all that antagonism pouring out and nobody there. She was not hurting anybody else. It certainly wasn't bothering her husband.

I am not defending the man. He was wrong. We all are confronted by people who are thoughtless and inconsiderate. Fortunately joy depends upon our communion with God. This is a tremendous thought, a gem, a jewel.

She asked, "Would you act joyfully if your wife did that to you?"

"It would depend on my spiritual condition," I replied.

That lady did not need sympathy. She needed to be shown a way out. All she wanted to do was to talk about how wrong her husband was. What she needed to do was recognize how wrong she was. Of course he was wrong, but her misery was not caused by his behavior. Her problem was under her own skin. His behavior triggered the furious anger in her heart. Only God can cleanse that heart. Then she can walk in the Spirit and enjoy life independent of other people's choices or the events of the day.

What separates people from God? You know the simple answer: sin.

Three things can be said about anyone who is seething, furious, angry, hateful—all alone in a room:

1. The problem is going on underneath the skin.
2. This problem was triggered by someone or some event outside of this person.
3. The incident has triggered a bodily condition that is intolerable.

Look at this problem compared to a list of sins. Which sins apply?

> **All unrighteousness is sin, and there is sin not leading to death.**
>
> 1 JOHN 5:17

> **Therefore, to him who knows to do good and does not do it, to him it is sin.**
>
> JAMES 4:17

> **Let all bitterness, wrath, anger, clamor, and evil speaking be put away from you, with all malice.**
>
> EPH. 4:31

> **He who despises his neighbor sins;**
> **But he who has mercy on the poor, happy is he.**
>
> PROV. 14:21

> **But if you show partiality, you commit sin, and are convicted by the law as transgressors.**
>
> JAMES 2:9

> **The devising of foolishness is sin,**
> **And the scoffer is an abomination to men.**
>
> PROV. 24:9

> **"For rebellion is as the sin of witchcraft,**
> **And stubbornness is as iniquity and idolatry"**
>
> 1 SAM. 15:23

But the wicked are like the troubled sea,
When it cannot rest,
Whose waters cast up mire and dirt.
"There is no peace,"
Says my God, "for the wicked."

ISA. 57:20–21

"The heart is deceitful above all things,
And desperately wicked;
Who can know it?"

JER. 17:9

Whoever commits sin also commits lawlessness, and sin is
lawlessness.

1 JOHN 3:4

Sin affects the way you act, speak, react, think, and your purpose in life. You can add to these definitions of sin and use them as a kind of spiritual magnifying glass to help point out sin.

Redemptive preaching and redemptive conversations will help your audiences to identify their own sins. You can teach people to think about the place of sin in their lives. If they do not have peace, you may conclude that wickedness is involved (Isa. 57:21).

Levels of Wickedness

There are levels of wickedness. For example, a teenager tells his mother he is going to the library. Instead he goes to meet his girlfriend. That is wickedness. But it is not as wicked as the man who tells his wife he must go to the office tonight and meets another woman. I do not think it is as wicked to swipe a nickel out of your mother's purse as it is to rob a bank. Nevertheless, all of these

> *If they do not have peace, you may conclude that wickedness is involved.*

acts were cut from the same cloth. They come from the same heart. God says that there is no peace to the wicked. He is a high enough authority.

Some Christians complain that "the heavens are like brass"—they pray yet it does not help. I am reminded of some lines by Shakespeare:

My words fly up, my thoughts remain below.
Words without thoughts never to heaven go.

A man told me that he had been on his knees weeping and agonizing all night in prayer, and it did not work. This man should approach God on His terms. Isaiah 59:1–2 gives a glimpse of God's terms:

Behold, the LORD's hand is not shortened,
That it cannot save;
Nor His ear heavy,
That it cannot hear.
But your iniquities have separated you from your God;
And your sins have hidden His face from you,
So that He will not hear.

You may not want to meet God's terms. Some people ask me how can I be made to want to? No one can make you want to, nor do you need to want to. You can choose to turn to God just as well as you can choose not to. That is your privilege. This is freedom.

There is great hope there because you can do something about your sin. You cannot do anything about your husband or your wife, but you can do something about yourself. These are wonderful truths. Scatter them as widely as you can while you preach and while you help people. Do not let Satan get you in a corner with a small handful of people who do not want help.

It is a needy world. We need many pastors preaching redemptively in the pulpits with a cheerful gleam in their eyes, backed up with a pure heart.

It should be further noted that people who have never studied the Bible, but are very sincere and dedicated to helping people, do not describe people the way the Bible does. Most psychologists believe that people are basically good, and if we will create proper conditions, pressures, and training around them, it will release the good that is within them.

The Bible says that man is basically evil and needs a change of heart. He needs to be born again. He needs some resources outside himself, and these resources come from God. So as far as I am concerned, I accept the nature of man as learned out of the Bible, and counsel people accordingly.

The Law of Sin and the Law of the Spirit

A law that tends to pull us downward is called the *law of sin*. A law that tends to pull us upward is called the *law of the Spirit of life in Christ Jesus*.

We all want to be kind, considerate, understanding, and easy going. We would like to be people who overlook others' faults, generous, even tempered. Each of us is confronted with a law most aptly described by the apostle Paul:

> **For the good that I will to do, I do not do; but the evil I will not to do, that I practice. Now if I do what I will not to do, it is no longer I who do it, but sin that dwells in me.**
>
> Rom. 7:19–20

We make the best of resolves, we have the best of intentions, and we miss the mark.

Evil may be something drastic like robbing a bank or committing adultery or murder. It could also be our reaction to little things, like the way an employee keeps his desk, or the way your husband drives, or the way your wife treats the cat, the way your child keeps his room, the way your neighbor keeps his yard. Just ordinary everyday things. We find that these little things bring out of us reactions, feelings, impulses that are unacceptable even to ourselves. We make an issue out of a situation although we would rather overlook it. We speak harshly although we would rather speak kindly. We think unwholesome thoughts although we would rather think positive thoughts. In other words, we missed the mark that we had privately set for ourselves. Isn't that so? The marks that we set for ourselves need not be words or deeds; they can be our own private world of thoughts, feelings, emotions, or desires. It is the unexpected circumstances that often brings out this law of sin within us.

There is an answer from the Scriptures for whoever asks the question sincerely: "Who will set me free from the clutches of my own sinful nature?"

Anyone who wishes to understand the sinful nature can do so:

> **Therefore by the deeds of the law no flesh will be justified in His sight, for by the law [is] the knowledge of sin.**
>
> Rom. 3:20

The key to correcting the sinful nature is found in another law:

> For what the law could not do in that it was weak through the flesh, God did by sending His own Son in the likeness of sinful flesh, on account of sin: He condemned sin in the flesh, that the righteous requirement of the law might be fulfilled in us who do not walk according to the flesh but according to the Spirit.
>
> ROM. 8:3–4

We need to linger a while and relish the possibility of the fruit of the Spirit available on demand. Can you imagine an infinite supply like this?

> The fruit of the Spirit is love, joy, peace, patience, kindness, goodness, faithfulness, gentleness, and self-control. Against such things there is no law.
>
> GAL. 5:22, NIV

You cannot pass a law that forces me to love you, to have a joyful heart, a peaceful spirit. You can force me to *act* loving, joyful, peaceful. However, the outward appearance is not an indicator of the condition under the skin.

The fruit of the Spirit, after all, is not the result of interacting with people or circumstances. It is the result of a relationship with God. There is a process involved in moving from control by the sinful nature to control of the Spirit. It involves some choices that you must make.

> And do not present your members as instruments of unrighteousness to sin, but present yourselves to God as being alive from the dead, and your members as instruments of righteousness to God.
>
> ROM. 6:13

According to 1 John 1:9 we are capable of yielding ourselves. What must we yield?

> If we confess our sins, He is faithful and just to forgive us our sins and to cleanse us from all unrighteousness.

If you are truly repentant, admit you are wrong, quit blaming someone else, and ask God for forgiveness and cleansing, God will answer your prayer. True repentance leads to feeling forgiven, cleansed, restored, renewed. Let Jesus break the law of sin in your body.

The fruit of the Spirit are the qualities that we seek, even in the face of stresses and strains and unexpected events. In other words, we do not produce a consistent pattern of such behavior through determination, willpower, self-control, or good intentions. You can test this out for yourself; you do not need to take my word for it. You can observe yourself and pay attention to your reactions.

The apostle Paul put it this way:

> **For it is God who works in you both to will and to do for His good pleasure.**
>
> PHIL. 2:13

Consistent living, then, is a matter of recognizing our own personal inability to produce that kind of response even though we want it. It involves yielding and receiving into our lives the ingredient that is lacking—the Spirit of Christ. As a counselor, I talk to many people who steadfastly keep up proper speech and conduct, but they do not have the spirit to match.

Paul strived to:

> **be found in Him, not having my own righteousness, which is from the law, but that which is through faith in Christ, the righteousness which is from God by faith.**
>
> PHIL. 3:9

That is what we need. I am not suggesting that we throw away laws. We must seek the Spirit who will enable us to conform to a reasonable law so that what we are saying and doing is a reflection of what is on our hearts and help others do the same.

HENRY T. BLACKABY

The pastor and the people of God whom he shepherds hold in their hands God's full provision for all of life's problems. *God has chosen for it to be that way. Jesus said He had given to us "the keys of the kingdom of heaven" (Matt. 16:19).* The pastor has the revelation of God to guide and help him "diagnose" the real problems he sees in people who seek his help. The Holy Spirit, who enables the pastor to fulfill his assignment to represent God to men, is always present and active in the pastor's life.

> **"But the Helper, the Holy Spirit, whom the Father will send in My name, He will teach you all things, and bring to your remembrance all things that I said to you."**
>
> JOHN 14:26

> **"However, when He, the Spirit of truth, has come, He will guide you into all truth."**
>
> JOHN 16:13

> **Now then, we are ambassadors for Christ, as though God were pleading through us: we implore you on Christ's behalf, be reconciled to God.**
>
> 2 COR. 5:20

The Holy Spirit assists the pastor to go beyond the "surface symptoms" to the root cause. The result is assurance that God is working in the life of the person to help him not only want to know God's provision but receive it as well. What a blessing a pastor can be to those in need.

Since the world does not believe in God, they leave people comforted but still in their sin.

In my ministry, I have come alongside many who were thinking about suicide. Each person was different. Their reason for wanting to take their life sprang from completely different circumstances and emotions. Only the Spirit of God, teaching us and guiding us to all truth, can reveal to us the heart of such a needy person. But, this is precisely what He does.

One day I was called to a young adult's home. She had said, nervously, that she was in great distress and had overwhelming urges to take her own life. I had not been speaking with her long after arriving at her house, than the Spirit urged me to ask her if she had ever dabbled with any occult practices. For I said, "Satan always moves a person to death, not life." She looked surprised at my question but freely shared how she had indeed practiced palm reading, astrology, used tarot cards, and other such practices.

I went to God's Word confident the Spirit of God had made known her real problem. Sure enough, as she confessed each practice, repented and forsook each one, and asked for the Spirit of God to fill her life, she was wonderfully set free—permanently, just as Jesus had promised!

Another significant gift God has given the pastor is a thorough knowledge of the Word of God. We know that

> **the word of God is living and powerful, and sharper than any two-edged sword, piercing even to the division of soul and spirit, and of joints and marrow, and is a discerner of the thoughts and intents of the heart. And there is no creature hidden from His sight, but all things are naked and open to the eyes of Him to whom we must give account.**
>
> HEB. 4:12–13

The world does not believe in or use the Word of God, so they usually deal with the relieving of "symptoms." They have no power to deal with root causes—namely, *sin*. Only God can deal with sin. Since the world does not believe in God, they leave people comforted but still in their sin.

REAL CAUSES AND REAL CURES

A pastor deals with root causes and provides people real cures. I spoke with a young doctor whom I had led to the Lord, and who was now an active member of our church.

I asked, "How do doctors approach medicine and people's needs?"

He said, "The philosophy of the medical profession is that we can heal, never; we can relieve, sometimes; we can comfort, always." He then added, "As a Christian, I also bring to their life, my God, who loves them and can do for them what we doctors cannot do. He also enables *me* to do what I cannot do without Him."

How incredible that God has made His enabling power available, not only to pastors but to His people as well—the Word of God! One clear word from God and all can be changed.

My wife, Marilynn, and I have often faced deeply hurting and bewildered people when we share how God healed our daughter of cancer. Many have said (often with a tone of bitterness), "I'm glad your daughter lived. Our child died!" At moments like this, our hearts immediately go out in love and compassion to them. I seek to turn them to God's Word—His Truth can set them free—and when He sets them free they are "free indeed" (John 8:36). I show them the Scriptures that speak so clearly of God's love for them (Rom. 5:1–10; John 3:16–17; 1 John 3:16). I then tell how God came to us and said,

- "Would you love Me just as much if I took her, or healed her?"
- "Where did I forever say, 'I love you'? In My Cross! Do not face anything in your life except against the backdrop of the Cross. My Cross (love) will never change because of circumstances."
- "My Cross and Resurrection are for just such times as these."

Then I may read to them 1 Corinthians 15:19–20, 50–56 concerning the assurance of our resurrection.

The Holy Spirit guides me specifically to Scriptures that bring release, hope, and joy, often immediately. I have literally seen the countenance and the lives change before my eyes as God's Word penetrates the mind, then the heart, then the will, and then the entire life.

BRINGING PEOPLE TO GOD

I was at a conference center when a young mother in her thirties came to me and shared how all three of her children had died, at different times, and that she could no longer have children. Then she began to share how Scripture flooded her mind and heart, and literally set her free. She said she still hurt over the loss; but she added, "Henry, the Scriptures assure me I have not lost them—they have preceded me to heaven, and I will spend eternity loving them. God has given me peace and joy, and now an expanding ministry to help others who have lost children and don't know where to turn to for peace. I turn them to God through His Word. Thank you for being my friend and helping me experience this in my life!"

A pastor and a church family can always bring their God to hurting people. What a privilege! What a real blessing we can be to others.

Grace and peace be multiplied to you in the knowledge of God and of Jesus our Lord, as His divine power has given to us all things that *pertain* to life and godliness, through the

knowledge of Him who called us by glory and virtue, by which have been given to us exceedingly great and precious promises, that through these you may be partakers of the divine nature, having escaped the corruption *that is* in the world through lust.

2 PET. 1:2-4

DOING WHAT THE FLESH CANNOT DO

It is so instructive for pastors to be reminded of how Paul saw his life in the midst of his world:

There is therefore now no condemnation to those who are in Christ Jesus, who do not walk according to the flesh, but according to the Spirit. For the law of the Spirit of life in Christ Jesus has made me free from the law of sin and death. For what the law could not do in that it was weak through the flesh, God did by sending His own Son in the likeness of sinful flesh, on account of sin: He condemned sin in the flesh, that the righteous requirement of the law might be fulfilled in us who do not walk according to the flesh but according to the Spirit.

ROM. 8:1-4

What the flesh cannot do, God does, through Christ! There is nothing in society to equal a pastor and a church, indwelt by God, with the resources of God fully available for every life, and every family, and every need.

Awesome is the power and presence of God to bring healing and hope in a sinful and hurting world. I have always known the incredible resources of God residing in a church family. While pastoring in Sasketoon, Saskatchewan, Canada, I sought to prepare our church family to be ready with compassion to bring God's resources to hurting people. One day we heard how two young men had murdered a Royal Canadian Mounted Policeman. This crime is very serious to people in Canada. In a prayer meeting that week, a fine couple said to us all, "We know what it is like to be the parents of young men who commit crime—the pain, the public scorn and rejection, the anger, and the tears. Would you pray for us, for we are going to find the parents of these two boys, visit them, and invite them to our home for coffee."

We prayed. They did, and both families came and said, "We have had rocks thrown at our house, been cursed, and deeply hurt. You are the only people who have expressed understanding, kindness, and help. Thanks!"

Our church learned afresh that God has placed in us His wonderful resources to heal a broken world. Out of this moment, our church began an ongoing ministry in the prisons, especially in the youth prison, and later began a ministry with the police department.

God always sees much deeper than we do and helps us understand the symptoms, and helps us deal with the root cause—sin. When sin is dealt with, a person is

> **a new creation; old things have passed away; behold, all things have become new.**
>
> 2 COR. 5:17

Only God through God's people can offer such a life-transforming difference. God has already provided fully for sin—and at an awful cost! And God's salvation is thorough, real, and personal. And we dare not "neglect so great a salvation" (Heb. 2:3), nor should we receive such grace of God "in vain" (2 Cor. 6:1–2).

TAPPING GOD'S RESOURCES

Pastor, you hold in your hand God's full provision for people's sins. Further, you are a worker together with God (2 Cor. 6:1). So you can speak to every person

> **as though God were pleading through us: we implore you on Christ's behalf, be reconciled to God.**
>
> 2 COR. 5:20

What huge things does God already have planned for the people and the community you serve?

> **But God has revealed them to us through His Spirit. For the Spirit searches all things, yes, the deep things of God.**
>
> 1 COR. 2:10

**For I know the thoughts that I think toward you, says the
LORD, thoughts of peace and not of evil, to give you a future
and a hope.**

JER. 29:11

Do not hesitate or avoid speaking for God! Do not hesitate to share
God's provision for every person's SIN. Know the Scriptures, and share
the Scriptures, letting the Holy Spirit guide you. The Spirit of God and
the Word of God will do their own work in each person. And God
wants to do this through your life, and your church—and your relationship with God and a hurting, seeking people.

A man named Don called me and asked if I could help him. He said
he had spoken to four pastors, and three said I would help him. He had a
problem with alcohol. Alcoholics Anonymous had told him he would
always be an alcoholic. I shared that when men help, they are very lim-
ited, and can really only comfort. But I assured him God could not only
help him, but cure him. I said this not on my word, but on God's Word. I
was simply His servant and could help this man to experience God's help.

The man walked about four miles to my home. When he arrived he
told me that when he was phoning me earlier, he was on the window
sill of the fourth floor of a hotel. If I had put him off, or said I could not
help him, he was going to jump to his death. I was his friend, and
shared from God's Word. A short time later, I was present when God
radically saved him. He never again touched alcohol. He became a
member of the church, a faithful usher, and a good friend.

The world said they could not cure, only comfort. God said,

**Moreover the law entered that the offense might abound.
But where sin abounded, grace abounded much more.**

ROM. 5:20

**A man has joy by the answer of his mouth,
And a word *spoken* in due season, how good it is!**

PROV. 15:23

**A word fitly spoken *is like* apples of gold
In settings of silver. *Like* an earring of gold and an ornament
of fine gold
Is a wise rebuker to an obedient ear.
Like the cold of snow in time of harvest**

Is a faithful messenger to those who send him
For he refreshes the soul of his masters.

Prov. 25:11–13

For I will give you a mouth and wisdom which all your adversaries will not be able to contradict or resist.

Luke 21:15

It was absolutely true to Don, and he was free—in Christ!

THINK SCRIPTURE—SHARE SCRIPTURE

Pastor, when you speak with hurting people, think Scripture and share Scripture. You really do not have an option as God's servant to His people—with God's message of "good news." Let God bring healing and wholeness to the lives of those seeking Him for His answers, through you.

I have rarely met persons in their home, at their work place, along the way, or in the activities of the church, with whom I was not thinking and sharing Scriptures. I was very focused to bring God's provision to His people at all times, and in all places. A pastor who did this was Richard Baxer. I suggest you read his classic book, *The Reformed Pastor.*

When God spoke to me some incredible truth that was changing me, I immediately sought every opportunity to share Him with everyone I met—especially fellow believers. I guided them to share with others their Savior who had and was bringing them to completeness in Christ (Col. 1:24–29). God had given me what the world did not have to share. I was excited about God's assignment for me to share God's Grace with others. And so often, what I shared with God's people, they would share with others. Later they would tell me how they had shared the truth with someone else, and God changed that person's life too!

God intends healing to come through His body, the church. You, personally, do not have all that people need—but God does, through His people.

PROCESS THE MESSAGE

1. Do you have such a love-relationship with God that you have a fresh word for those that are weary?

2. If you critiqued your own language, would you consider it to be biblically God-centered or more defined by the world's terminology? (i.e., Would you call lust an "addiction to sex" or a "work of the flesh"?)

3. How much do you inform the body of Christ of the problems within the church?

4. Do you remember some situations in the church where you have seen God use you as His messenger to bring wholeness to the body? Meditate on what God did so that it will encourage you to respond as God's servant to "speak a word in season to those that are weary" in the next difficulty.

5. In your counseling do you find yourself treating symptoms and simply comforting people? Or do you really offer them a cure by treating the problem?

6. What are you doing to enhance your knowledge of God's Word so that you can be of greater help to those who need it?

7. Do you find it easier to use worldly methods or spiritual truth in helping people? Why?

PART THREE

God's Standard for Your Heart

Keep Your Heart— Maintaining a Vital Inner Life

> *Keep your heart with all diligence,*
> *For out of it spring the issues of life.*
> PROVERBS 4:23
>
> *The minister needs to think of himself as a redemptive*
> *shepherd who can instruct people to turn to God*
> *for forgiveness and cleansing of sin and how to walk*
> *in the Spirit.*
> HENRY BRANDT
>
> *God examines the heart, knowing that good and evil things*
> *come from it. And the one God is looking for is the one*
> *whose heart is like His and His Son's.*
> HENRY T. BLACKABY

HENRY BRANDT

Strange. The ministerial voice that beckons the wounded, suffering soul to come look Godward for help gets weaker and weaker. Another voice called therapy gets louder and louder. The therapists' voices belong to the psychiatrist and the psychologist, who are becoming more and more skilled at helping people live with their sins.

The minister needs to think of himself as a redemptive shepherd who can instruct people to turn to God for forgiveness and cleansing of sin and how to walk in the Spirit. If the minister is to be one who can instruct God's people, he must maintain his own inner spiritual life with the Lord Jesus. As he does, he will be able to preach the truth in love.

Redemptive Preaching for the Inner Life

Your preaching should be provocative enough so that it makes people aware of their *total* selves. Oh, yes, it is a good thing for a person to be aware of his or her abilities, talents, and qualities. But it is equally important that we make people aware of their failings, their weaknesses, and their faults. I say it is positive to eliminate the negative. To do that, people need to become aware of what is negative—sin. If you want to have people searching their hearts, your message has to zero in on what is wrong.

> *If I can help*
> *someone*
> *identify his sin,*
> *I have done him*
> *a great favor.*

The process of identifying that which is negative in a person's life is not pleasant. You and I know man is sinful, but the blood of Jesus Christ can cleanse us of our sin. That is really oversimplification to many people. But the wonder of the gospel is that it is that simple! If I can help someone identify his sin, I have done him a great favor.

Intemperance—Gluttony—Sin

Our goal is healing. Our goal is redemptive. Reflecting on the following Bible verse proved to have redemptive value when I shared my thoughts in a meeting:

> **And let us consider one another in order to stir up love and good works.**
>
> HEB. 10:24

A redemptive opportunity developed for me at one of those family-style banquets where they pass the platters of food and you eat whatever you want. I was sitting next to the minister. He filled his plate with a pile of potatoes, smothered it with gravy and all the trimmings, and ate it all. That is not what impressed me. He did it all over again! I could not get my eyes off that second plate.

Finally, he leaned over to me and whispered, "You know, Doc (You whisper these things to psychologists—they understand.), I am a compulsive eater."

What is a redemptive answer to that? You cannot blame a man for being a compulsive eater, can you? I do not pass this way very often, so I wanted to give him a helpful answer.

I said, "Sir, I think there is a better word for it than that. It is called *intemperance*."

That is a provocative thought, is it not?

I continued: "With reference to food, there is even a more drastic word than that—*gluttony*. There is an even more drastic word than that—*sin*."

He smiled and finished his plate, but he was stirred up, spurred on, disturbed. I heard from his wife that he was very disturbed. The next time I saw the man was when he invited me to a banquet in his church a year later. He had slimmed down. He looked great. There we sat— this time it was a redemptive opportunity for the pastor. He leaned over to me and said, "Doc, you are heavier than you were a year ago."

I explained, "Yes, I cannot resist food."

He said, "There is a better word for it. The word is *intemperance*, and with reference to food there is even a better word than that. It is *gluttony*. There is an even better word. It is called sin."

That fellow stirred me. Whenever I head his way, I pay attention to my weight. When I see him, I size him up, believe me.

We need each other. Your people need to be reminded of what is right and wrong. You can do it from the pulpit. It takes a happy man communicating these wonderful truths—not an angry, bitter, rebellious man.

Our goal and objective, then, is to make people conscious of their qualities and their liabilities and weaknesses. We must help people to realize that life stimulates whatever is in you—good or bad.

THE PASTOR'S INNER LIFE

If your goal is to be alert to redemptive opportunities, you must pay close attention to your own spiritual life.

> **"Only take heed to yourself, and diligently keep yourself lest you forget the things your eyes have seen, and lest they depart from your heart all the days of your life. And teach them to your children and your grandchildren."**
>
> DEUT. 4:9

Pay attention to your heart. Pay attention to where your hope is, lest you forget what your eyes have seen. This facet of human nature (neglecting your heart) can short-circuit your love and your intelligence. I find that the smarter people are, the more brilliant are their rationalizations and the evil that they get into. The brilliant person can kick up a bigger fuss than an average person. Perverted intelligence is dangerous. It divides families, churches, and denominations. Take heed unto yourself. Pay attention to your character. Pay attention to how you are responding to people, lest you forget all that you have learned.

> *I find that the smarter people are, the more brilliant are their rationalizations and the evil that they get into.*

What goes on underneath your skin? You can come up to me with a friendly smile and tell me how great you feel, even though you do not. You can act and look like a Christian and develop a pastoral manner so that nobody in the congregation would have a flicker of a hint that you are anything but a happy man. I hope that is not your goal. Watch yourself closely.

Nathaniel Hawthorne said, "No man for any considerable period can wear one face to himself and another to the multitude without finally getting bewildered as to which may be true." People are not quite sure who they are if they are wearing several faces.

A seminary professor had a severe, painful case of colitis. His physician said it was psychosomatic. The professor was irritated with some of his students who were resisting the teaching that he gave them. He was irritated at some of the policies of the seminary, and irritated at his wife. Life was just one big irritation. As we talked I tried to point out that his response to life was wrong. What he called dedication was plain, ordinary hostility and stubbornness. I do not know how else to call a man stubborn and hostile except to say, "You are stubborn and hostile." I knew he was hostile because when I told him that he got mad. A very important part of this session was that I was not getting mad at him. I met him a year later, and he said, "I want you to know that one session I had with you was the greatest thing that ever happened to me, and I have not had any colitis since." This was a spiritual, redemptive encounter.

> **Beloved, I pray that you may prosper in all things and be in health, just as your soul prospers.**
>
> 3 JOHN 2

Spiritual Deception

As a group, ministers are wholesome people. I am by way of warning, or maybe helping, simply illustrating the fact that ministers' knowledge can get short-circuited. "The heart is deceitful" (Jer. 17:9). The deception of the human heart is not cleared away by education. We have a tremendous capacity for self-deception, so systematic that psychologists have catalogued the various forms—regression, repression, suppression, and rationalization.

A friend of mine has this hanging on his wall:

> Persistent dependability is appreciated by everyone. A brilliant display of ability and occasional flashes of genius are seriously discounted if the follow-through of reliable character is lacking.

A brilliant candidate sermon is fine, but when you start living with the people your behavior must support and reassure them that your sermon was not just a flash. Those who are outstanding under the tension of an emergency and who at the same time prove reliable in the long, strong, steady pull are the ones upon whom great responsibility can be placed with confidence.

A Redemptive Conversation

A pastor suffering from an ulcer wrote me a letter. He said he already had some counseling so he knew what his problem was but he wanted to come and talk to me about it. It seemed strange to me that a fellow would drive a thousand miles to tell me what he already knew, but he did. He came in that first session and started right in talking, telling me all about what he had learned from his therapy. He told me about his mother and father and how their problems affected him, and how his sisters and brothers affected him. The second day he came in and told me about his school and neighborhood and how they affected him. He still had not asked me if I wanted to know this. He came to the third session with his mouth open. About half way through I stopped him cold.

I said to him, "Do you know what you are doing?"

He hung his head and said, "Yes, sir, I know what I am doing. I am afraid of you."

How about that, afraid of a nice man like me? The man did have an ulcer, and it was psychosomatic.

I asked him, "Who are you mad at?" He was a seminary graduate, and this was his first church. He had learned in seminary that using the eye-gate is much more effective than using the eargate. He had learned in seminary how to evaluate a Sunday school, which is what he did. He found his church to be lacking. He prepared some graphs and charts and called the deacons together to present his case—why they needed to change the Sunday school. *It never occurred to him that anyone would question a presentation when you use both the eargate and the eyegate.*

One of the deacons said, "I have been in this church a long time and I do not see any reason for changing the Sunday school." They voted him down. He spent the result of the week sulking in his study. He called it "righteous indignation." He saw another problem. They could certainly improve the atmosphere of worship if they at least had a part-time music director. The church refused his request. He resented the congregation. He would get up to preach and there were the people he resented.

> *The idea that if you cannot feel like a Christian, at least you can act like one, is one of the most dangerous ideas you can come up with.*

I said, "That is not right."

His reply was what I almost invariably expect: "Have you ever been a preacher?"

I would like to know what that has to do with it? Sometimes people wonder how you can understand if you have not experienced what they have gone through. Have you ever stopped to think what kind of training that would take? Why, you would need to be a thief, and a liar, and an adulterer. You would need to be divorced. You would need to beat up somebody. Would that not be a strange course? You do not need to experience what everybody experiences in order to understand them. What you need to know is what God is like and what the Bible says about it.

My minister counselee got a glimpse of himself and found the same thing happening to him that Jesus said happens to people:

> **And this is the condemnation, that the light has come into the world, and men loved darkness rather than light, because their deeds were evil. For everyone practicing evil hates the light and does not come to the light, lest his deeds should be exposed.**
>
> JOHN 3:19-20

My minister counselee was mad at his congregation. He was convinced that they caused him to be mad. I pointed out some Bible verses to him:

> **But now you yourselves are to put off all these: anger, wrath, malice, blasphemy, filthy language out of your mouth.**
>
> COL. 3:8

> **Do not lie to one other.**
>
> COL. 3:9

> **Therefore, as the elect of God, holy and beloved, put on tender mercies, kindness, humility, meekness, longsuffering; bearing with one another, and forgiving one another, if anyone has a complaint against another; even as Christ forgave you, so you also must do.**
>
> COL. 3:12–13

He would preach on Sunday with malice in his heart toward his people. Not only did he keep his feelings to himself, but he gave his congregation the impression that he loved them. He was getting comfortable with the self-deception that he must act loving even if he can not be loving.

After the service he would greet the people, "Good morning, I am glad to see you." At the same time that he was struggling with bitterness in his heart, he was polishing up his ability to be deceptive without being obvious about it. Let me warn you about that. The idea that if you cannot feel like a Christian, at least you can act like one, is one of the most dangerous ideas you can come up with.

He who covers his sins will not prosper,
But whoever confesses and forsakes them will have mercy.

PROV. 28:13

God's Resources for Heart Trouble

I do not know if you are an angry person or a bitter, stubborn, rebellious person. There is a possibility before you finish reading this book that you can experience a change of heart. The complexities of your background do not cut you off from God's resources—*nobody* can do that.

> *The complexities of your background do not cut you off from God's resources—* nobody *can do that.*

Most people would rather dwell on past history than search their hearts and confess their sins. Anger, wrath, malice, and lying are sins. That is a blow. It was a blow to my counselee. "You tell me I am sinful?" How would you answer that? My answer is, "Yes, sir." I do not get nervous with the word *sin*. My job is to diagnose it. Nursing malice in your heart toward someone can be pleasurable. For example, you may be studying and you get to thinking about somebody you do not like. The more you think about that person the madder you get. You think yourself into a frenzy all by yourself. It is pleasurable, is it not? Haven't you delighted in just thinking about telling somebody else how you feel about them?

Listen to this:

> For where envy and self-seeking exist, confusion and every evil thing are there.

JAMES 3:16

Is it not true that when we are angry a wrong act can sound so right? Is it not true that some of you have said things you surely wished you could call back even before you were halfway through saying them? Is it not true that some of you have done things you knew were wrong and now you wish it had not happened? Listen, when you have envy and strife in your heart, an evil deed can sound good. When a person has done wrong, look for envy and strife and selfish ambition in his heart. It will be there.

Dealing with Resistance

People come to see me and they want to talk about problems. I want to talk about the heart. Even though people will resist examining the heart, that does not mean they will not do it. We must learn to deal with resistance. Jesus said,

> **"And men loved darkness rather than light, because their deeds were evil.**
>
> JOHN 3:19

I read this verse to my minister friend. It "burned him up." When you expose yourself to the spotlight of the Bible, you tend to reject it, to push it away, to become antagonistic to the person who presented it. But I have not found a way of getting through to the heart of the matter without some resistance.

I advised this young minister, "Pay attention to your reactions while you are here." He came a thousand miles from a sleepy little Midwestern town where nobody is going anywhere, they ease up to a stop sign, look around, and ease along. You do not do that in my hometown of Detroit. We are in a hurry. He was driving along and a big eighteen-wheeler came booming down the highway behind him and let him have a blast on the horn. He did not like it. He became angry at somebody he would never meet. It is a sad state of affairs to respond in anger at the traffic. It began to dawn on this young man that there was something wrong within. We finally saw his burdens roll away as he was willing to ask the Lord to change his attitude

Life does not cause the condition of the heart; life reveals the condition of the heart.

toward those deacons, the congregation, toward me, and toward everybody. In other words, he had to come to the place where he could admit to God, "God, I am an angry, hostile person. I need help."

Life does not cause the condition of the heart; life reveals the condition of the heart. There is wisdom that comes from above that has nothing to do with people. It involves a relationship between you and God, and it will be available to you as you realize the condition of your own heart and your own helplessness.

Dimensions of the Works of the Flesh

There is uniformity about a person's response to life. Our job, if we are to do redemptive preaching, is to be clear about the nature of human response to life. Envy, anger, love, and joy are called emotions in the psychology book. In the Bible, envy and anger are called works of the flesh (sin), and love and joy are called a fruit of the Spirit. You will discover that if a person is not walking in the Spirit, then this person is walking in the flesh. In that condition, he or she will respond to life in a prescribed fashion. We need to take a look at the dimensions of the works of the flesh (or the acts of the sinful nature):

> **Now the works of the flesh are evident, which are: adultery, fornication, uncleanness, lewdness, idolatry, sorcery, hatred, contentions, jealousies, outbursts of wrath, selfish ambitions, dissensions, heresies, envy, murders, drunkenness, revelries, and the like; of which I tell you beforehand, just as I also told you in time past, that those who practice such things will not inherit the kingdom of God.**
>
> GAL. 5:19–21

Another word to describe this condition of the heart is sin. There is no human remedy. Jesus Christ died to save us from our sins. The Holy Spirit empowers us to walk in the Spirit.

A biblical description of a person's basic problem calls for a biblical solution:

> **I say then: Walk in the Spirit, and you shall not fulfill the lust of the flesh.**
>
> GAL. 5:16

> **But the fruit of the Spirit is love, joy, peace, longsuffering, kindness, goodness, faithfulness, gentleness, self-control. Against such there is no law.**
>
> GAL. 5:22–23

The solution is to look to God for His Spirit.

> **But the wisdom that is from above is first pure, then peaceable, gentle, willing to yield, full of mercy and good fruits, without partiality and without hypocrisy. Now the fruit of righteousness is sown in peace by those who make peace.**
>
> JAMES 3:17–18

My job was to help this minister realize this. After some resistance, he repented of his anger and yielded his life to walk in the Spirit.

The Biblical Solution

How did I help him? By listening to his story and comparing it to the Bible.

The following are perhaps the most important statements in this series:

1. There is no human remedy for the sinful nature.
2. There is no human source for the fruit of the Spirit.
3. Each person must approach God for help on God's terms.
4. God will help anyone who asks.
5. Our role is to declare that Jesus forgives us and cleanses us from sin; the Holy Spirit is the source of the fruit of the Spirit.
6. The condition of your heart does not and never did involve people.
7. Walking in the Spirit has nothing to do with people.

I remind you again that the fruit of the Spirit is love, joy, peace, long-suffering, gentleness, goodness, faith, meekness, and temperance. If these are not present, your relationship to God needs attention. An overwhelming number of the church body sincerely believe that the fruit of the Spirit is really triggered by a proper mix of people and events.

Christians are flocking to the divorce courts. I talk to many couples who assume that the right partner would turn on an internal love mechanism. It seems they have bought into the notion that a warm, friendly, gentle response toward their partner is the responsibility of the partner. The man says to me, "I lost my love." You lost your love! Where did you lose it? Let us go find it. "I have married the wrong woman." Then his young wife speaks. "I am disappointed. I thought this man would stir up warm, friendly, tender, kindly feelings in me. Instead, he leaves me cold." He does? "Do you suppose I married the wrong man?"

Anybody who gets married realizes very quickly that your heart is not transformed by a person—because no person will change your heart. "Why am I so antagonistic toward my wife? How can I change her life so that my good qualities can come out of me?" It is not your wife. The source of love is Godward. You see, having the fruit of the Spirit in your life does not have anything to do with people. Did not the Scripture say that the fruit of the Spirit involves a relationship between you and God? We try to change the human heart by juggling rules and regulations, insight and understanding.

If the problem involves the flesh, there is no human remedy. There is human relief. Humanist therapists can help you manage your sins. If walking in the Spirit is the answer, there is no human remedy. Only God can help you. This is the good news. He will help anyone who sincerely asks.

The great need of the day is to make people conscious of the products of their own hearts. Let us be careful to present a biblical solution. The Bible is sufficient to describe the works of the flesh and to prescribe the remedy.

HENRY T. BLACKABY

A Pastor's Character

The Scriptures clearly guide us to fullness of life by exhorting us:

> **Keep your heart with all diligence,**
> **For out of it spring the issues of life.**
>> PROV. 4:23

The Amplified Bible expresses it this way:

> **Keep and guard your heart with all vigilance and above all**
> **that you guard, for out of it flow the springs of life.**
>> PROV. 4:23, AMP

The Scriptures go on to indicate some of what this would mean, in the very next verses:

> **Put away from you false and dishonest speech, and willful**
> **and contrary talk put far from you. Let your eyes look right**

on [with fixed purpose] and let your gaze be straight before you. Consider well the path of your feet, and let all your ways be established and ordered aright. Turn not aside to the right hand or to the left; remove your foot from evil.

PROV. 4:24–27, AMP

When the apostle Paul set out the character, or heart condition, required of a pastor, he used these words:

A bishop then must be blameless, the husband of one wife, temperate, sober-minded, of good behavior, hospitable, able to teach.

1 TIM. 3:2

This is a tall order, but it is crucial to the life of a pastor. Let me go on to give what else Paul said:

. . . circumspect and temperate and self-controlled; [he must be] sensible and well behaved and dignified and lead an orderly (disciplined) life; [he must be] hospitable [showing love for and being a friend to the believers, especially strangers and foreigners and be] a capable and qualified teacher. . . not combative but gentle and considerate, not quarrelsome but forbearing and peaceable, and not a lover of money [insatiable for wealth and ready to obtain it by questionable means]. He must rule his own household well, keeping his children under control, with true dignity, commanding their respect in every way and keeping them respectful. . . . Furthermore he must have a good reputation and be well thought of by those outside [the church], lest he become involved in slander and incur reproach and fall into the devil's trap.

1 TIM. 3:2–5, 7, AMP

These qualities are the outcome of his character. His character is his heart. The condition of our heart is in our hands and cannot be affected by things from the outside. We can "stand guard over our heart," keeping it with all diligence—because out of our heart flows our life. God examines the heart, knowing that good and evil things come from it. And the one God is looking for is the one whose heart is like His and His Son's.

A Reflection of Time Spent with God

We guard our heart by keeping a very close relationship with our Lord. The apostles knew this and asked the church to select and appoint seven men full of the Holy Spirit, faith, and wisdom to take care of the heavy responsibilities of the day-to-day needs of the people and maintain unity in the church family. The apostles could then give themselves "continually to prayer and to the ministry of the word" (Acts 6:4). The inner life of the apostles was vital to the spiritual health of the church. The future of God's purpose to redeem a lost world hung in the balance. As would go the church in Jerusalem, so would go the plan of God to have His people be

"witnesses to Me in Jerusalem, and in all Judea and Samaria, and to the end of the earth."

ACTS 1:8

The teaching and preaching to the new believers was critical! Prayer and the ministry of the Word were essential to that process. The lives of the apostles were imperative in it all. The hearts of the apostles were kept pure and clean before God and His people by prayer and the Scriptures. Any neglect here, even in the slightest degree, would have immeasurable consequences. Just as clearly as the future of Israel in the Old Testament depended on Moses receiving every word from God, so would it be with God's people in Jerusalem whom God had appointed to carry the gospel to all nations.

And this is emphatically true in our day. The redemption of our nation and the nations of the world rests upon the fullness of relationship of God's people with their Lord. And the pastors of our day carry this responsibility preeminently. Pastor, your time in prayer and the Scriptures, and the ministry of those Scriptures to God's people in the enabling of the Holy Spirit, cannot be understated! Nothing must interfere with or turn us aside from this. Our character rests on both the quality and the quantity of our time with God in prayer and Scripture.

So often, what God does to me and with me in my time with Him affects dramatically

- what I share;
- who hears it;
- the effect of God's specific Word in their lives.

I was speaking from God's Word at an "Experiencing God for Couples" conference in Texas. Marilynn, my wife, was speaking with me, and we had shared and prayed about our time. A fine couple approached us and said God had deeply spoken to them and they were processing it all before the Lord. The husband told me he was a circuit court judge. We prayed together. I was grateful I had spent time in prayer and the ministry of God's Word. A year later, Marilynn and I were doing a similar conference in another state. This circuit court judge was waiting to see me. He said, "Henry, let me tell you what God has been doing since we spoke with you a year ago. I am now enrolled in seminary, am pastoring a little church, am still a circuit court judge, and next Saturday I will be ordained to the ministry. Thank you for your faithfulness."

A Reflection of an Intimate Relationship with God

Nothing is more vital to a pastor's care of the flock than his own personal inner life. All the qualities listed by Paul to young Timothy are the fruit of the heart that walks with God. The fruit of the Spirit, as Henry Brandt pointed out earlier, is love, joy, peace, longsuffering, kindness, goodness, faithfulness, gentleness, and self-control. Pastor, are these present and real and obvious to your people in your life right now? If not, you are not walking in the Spirit. Remember, these are not optional in the pastor's life, these are essential. The apostle John put it wonderfully in 1 John 1:7 when he said

> **if we [really] are living and walking in the Light, as He [Himself] is in the Light, we have [true, unbroken] fellowship with one another, and the blood of Jesus Christ His Son cleanses (removes) us from all sin and guilt [keeps us cleansed from sin in all its forms and manifestations].**
>
> **AMP**

There is no substitute for this intimate relationship with God. "Walking" means "as a way of life." This is what Abraham did. So intimate and life-encompassing was this that it is said of him

> **"Abraham believed God, and it was accounted to him for righteousness." And he was called the friend of God.**
>
> **JAMES 2:23**

It was said of Moses

So the LORD spoke to Moses face to face, as a man speaks to his friend.

EXOD. 33:11

It is no different today. Character that God blesses and uses is shaped in prolonged *koinonia* (fellowship) with God, walking in the light of His presence—in holiness and completeness in Christ.

The apostles knew how significant this was, for they had spent three and a half years in just such a relationship with Jesus. Now they continued in prayer and the Scriptures, under the intimate presence and guidance of the Spirit of God. They knew that if they "walked in the Spirit" they would not fulfill the lust of the flesh (Gal. 5:16; Rom. 8:5–14).

Everything in the pastor's life and ministry flows out of the condition of the heart. There is nothing that I have sought to give more diligent attention to in my life as a pastor, and as a husband and father, than the spiritual condition of my heart. And there is nothing that I know of that I have seen that leads to the "fall," or destruction, of a pastor's life and ministry any more tragically than inattention to the inner life.

> *All the counsel and instruction we may give to others will have no integrity if our own personal relationship with God is lacking.*

This is not merely a matter of maintaining a "daily quiet time." It is far deeper than that. It is a matter of character, developed by constant fellowship with our Lord, and our Heavenly Father, aided by the Holy Spirit. This is a twenty-four-hour-a-day relationship, carefully maintained and nourished. All the counsel and instruction we may give to others will have no integrity if our own personal relationship with God is lacking.

Let me carefully and lovingly suggest that the God-given assignment of the pastor is not as a CEO, or as an administrator, builder, treasurer, or planner. The pastor is to be in the midst of God's people, a "spiritual pace-setter," guide, and teacher.

God Himself said to Ezekiel,

> **For they are impudent and stubborn children. I am sending you to them, and you shall say to them, "Thus says the Lord GOD." As for them, whether they hear or whether they refuse—for they are a rebellious house—yet they will know that a prophet has been among them.**
>
> EZEK. 2:4–5

Paul also had as his goal and fully understood the importance of his heart and life before God and God's people when he said,

> **I now rejoice in my sufferings for you, and fill up in my flesh what is lacking in the afflictions of Christ, for the sake of His body, which is the church, of which I became a minister according to the stewardship from God which was given to me for you, to fulfill the word of God, the mystery which has been hidden from ages and from generations, but now has been revealed to His saints. To them God willed to make known what are the riches of the glory of this mystery among the Gentiles: which is Christ in you, the hope of glory. Him we preach, warning every man and teaching every man in all wisdom, that we may present every man perfect in Christ Jesus. To this end I also labor, striving according to His working which works in me mightily.**
>
> COL. 1:24–29

It would be costly to Paul to "present every man perfect in Christ Jesus," but that was God's assignment for his life. It must be every pastor's goal also. This was my goal as a pastor. This heart of Paul for God's people is seen in his prayer life, as revealed in these passages: Ephesians 1:15–23; 3:14–21; Philippians 1:9–11; Colossians 1:9–14. Study them and then examine the focus and intensity of your praying for God's people.

Of course, the prayer of Jesus in John 17 will always remain the pinnacle of intercession and a pattern for discipling prayer for every pastor. May our prayer lives reveal our passion for the people of God to become perfect in Christ!

P R O C E S S   T H E   M E S S A G E

1. Do you know anybody you do not like, somebody who gripes you, who annoys you?

2. Do you feel bitter, rebellious, stubborn?

3. Does your character match your message?

4. How would those closest to you (wife, children, friends) assess your character?

5. How is character being developed in your life?

6. Sharing messages with the people you lead can be influenced by how they are treating you. How do you pray for help in this area of life?

7. Do you know any pastors, missionaries, or other leaders who need your help? How will you help them?

8. Pastor, is the fruit of the Spirit present and real and obvious to your people in your life right now?

EIGHT

Obedience— The Basis for Personal Contentment

My little children, let us not love in word or in tongue, but in deed and in truth.
1 JOHN 3:18

I have been impressed across the years how easy it is for us to give lip service to our devotion to the Bible and then ignore it when it comes to a practical application in everyday life.
HENRY BRANDT

The source of peace and fulfillment in ministry is not conditioned by circumstances. Peace and fulfillment come from a sincere relationship with God, and our Lord Jesus Christ, who called us.
HENRY T. BLACKABY

HENRY BRANDT

A lawyer asked Jesus, "Master, which is the great commandment in the law?" If you were to pick just one commandment to live by, which one would it be? This is what Jesus said:

"You shall love the LORD your God with all your heart, with all your soul, and with all your mind." This is the first and great commandment.

MATT. 22:37–38

The foundation for personal happiness, more important than the appearance you make in society, is the relationship between you and God in the quietness of your own soul—your dedication to serving and pleasing Him.

OBEDIENCE TO GOD'S COMMANDMENTS

If it is my intent to love God as Jesus said I should, how would I go about it? Jesus gave a clue when He said to His disciples,

If you love Me, keep My commandments.
JOHN 14:15

To be in love with somebody like I was with my wife when we were courting was a wonderful experience. I dreamed about that girl. I talked about her all the time. I had trouble thinking about anything else. I could hardly wait to see her again. When a letter came from her it was opened immediately and read over and over. What wonderful days! I carried her picture in my wallet, and at odd moments I would take it out and gaze at it fondly. She gave me a picture for my dresser. I adored that picture. I loved to talk to her on the telephone. I drove fifteen miles to see her—seven nights a week, and twice on Saturday if she would let me. I spent all my money on her. I borrowed money to spend on her.

There were times, however, when I had to reconsider our courtship. She, too, had occasion to ponder her commitment. To please her often meant not pleasing myself. The demands of harmonizing two lives tends to push thoughts about God into the background.

Our relationship with God is similar. There are all the attractions in this world, reputations that you can make, jobs that you can get, money that you can earn, places you can go, and the things that you can acquire— how hard it is to keep your focus on God and His commandments!

I have been impressed across the years how easy it is for us to give lip service to our devotion to the Bible and then ignore it when it comes to a practical application in everyday life.

Many people come my way because they want to talk to a Christian. They come in with their heavy Bibles—big Bibles. Mind you, I am not against carrying one. I am saying that the person who ends up in the consulting room carrying a big Bible obviously does not know what is in that big book, or is not paying any attention to what is in it. Your knowledge of the Bible does not do you much good unless you practice it, just like your knowledge of the speed limit does not do you much good unless you obey it.

I used to teach in Chicago one day a week, commuting by air from Flint, Michigan. This one morning I got a late start so I was hurrying to the airport. (That's another way of saying that I was speeding!) I noted a car in my rearview mirror with this globe on top and the light going round and round. I thought to myself, *I had better move over. This guy is in a hurry!* He was after me! Between the time he got out of his car and walked to mine I had figured out an excuse.

He approached me and said in an understatement, "You were speeding."

"Yes, sir, I am a seminary professor and a psychologist and I am on my way to teach my class in Chicago, I got a late start and that is why I am speeding."

I was surprised at his response.

He said, "What! You mean to tell me that you are a professor and a psychologist and you are speeding down this street? If we cannot depend on people like you, who can we depend on?"

He took out his form and filled it out. He was not impressed at all by the fact that I was needed in Chicago. I did not get in trouble for a lack of knowledge or information; I got in trouble because I was not doing what I knew to do. That is true for many of us.

It is not your knowledge that produces closeness to the Lord, it is your *obedience*. Some people have memorized a hundred verses and spit them out at you, but they do not heed them. I will take the person who knows a few verses and lives by them. There can be a gap between what you know and what you *do*. There are many Christians who do not know or do not care to remember what they know about the Bible. Since their hearts are elsewhere, inevitable misery will be coming into their lives. It may not be visible to someone else. Most people who come to see me do so because of personal unhappiness that nobody knows about. They

> *It is not your knowledge that produces closeness to the Lord, it is your obedience.*

prefer misery instead of yielding to the resources that are available. Their treasure is elsewhere.

Spend Time in the Word

It is foundational that we meditate on the Bible, think about it, experiment with it, risk obeying it, and watch what happens to other people who try or do not try to obey it. We either illustrate the benefits of walking according to the Word or the penalties of not walking according to biblical principles. We simply prove what the Bible says and that is

> **Do not be deceived, God is not mocked; for whatever a man sows, that he will also reap.**
>
> GAL. 6:7

I am learning that the key to loving the people in my life is to keep Christ's commandments.

> **If you keep My commandments, you will abide in My love, just as I have kept My Father's commandments and abide in His love.**
>
> JOHN 15:10

Another glimpse of the benefit of loving God is this incredible view:

> **And may the Lord make you increase and abound in love to one another and to all, just as we do to you, so that He may establish your hearts blameless in holiness before our God and Father at the coming of our Lord Jesus Christ with all His saints.**
>
> 1 THESS. 3:12–13

The Bible is telling us that our sense of self-respect, contentment, and a clear conscience are directly related to loving God who is the source of love for people.

Love Yourself and Others

In answering the lawyer's question, Jesus spoke of the first and greatest commandment:

> **Jesus said to him, "'You shall love the LORD your God with all your heart, with all your soul, and with all your mind.'"**
>
> MATT. 22:37

He then spoke of the second commandment:

And *the* second *is* like it: "You shall love your neighbor as yourself."

MATT. 22:39

At first glance it is hard to see just how the two commandments are alike. Surely Jesus is not making a play on words. Then there must be a direct relationship between loving God and loving my neighbor as myself.

The Lord says that you cannot love anybody any more than you do yourself. That's fair enough. Your relationship to others can be a measure of what you think of yourself. So tonight when you close the door in your bedroom—and there isn't anybody around—walk up to the mirror, look yourself in the eye, and see if you can tell yourself, "I like what you said today. I like the tone of voice you used. I like what you thought. I like what you felt. I like the desires of your heart." This is the result of a deep-seated conviction that your behavior, your word, your thoughts, your feelings, and your desires are acceptable to the Lord.

It is hard to look yourself in the eye, especially when you have given somebody a tongue lashing, or you felt like it—wishing you had is just as bad as doing it.

For as he thinks in his heart, so is he.

PROV. 23:7

"For the Lord does not see as man sees; for man looks at the outward appearance, but the Lord looks at the heart."

1 SAM. 16:7

LIVING A LIE

A woman in great distress, seeking peace for her soul, told me her story: When she was twelve years old, her mother left her father for another man. Her father was an irresponsible drunkard. This twelve-year-old child, the oldest of six children, was faced with seeing the family broken up or assuming the responsibility of mother to the children. She assumed the responsibility and successfully managed to get through high school as well as take care of the family. Neighbors, teachers, church people, and the community helped. She kept the house and the children clean and neat, got them off to school, and made sure they went to church. Every Sunday the six of them marched down the aisle of the church, occupying the same pew. She received the plaudits and admiration of many for the fine, sacrificial job she did.

However, the girl deeply resented being placed in this position. She dreaded the dawning of every new day. This was her own little secret. She endured the task for seven years, then her father married again. She left home immediately, using the desire for higher education as the reason. In her heart she knew that she was laying down a task that she despised. The praise of the people only served to make her miserable. She knew that this praise was undeserved, because she was hiding an intense hatred toward her father and the children. The deepest desire of her heart had always been to flee the task and be like other girls. Neither her speech nor her actions betrayed her secret. Her hatred for her brothers and sisters spread to become hatred toward all children.

She married but refused to have children. Her husband could not understand. Her refusal had caused a deep rift in their marriage. At this point she decided that something must be done about her situation.

Her story illustrates the emptiness, the misery, the loneliness of words and actions that are out of line with our desires and feelings. What looked like ministering to others was not what it appeared to be. This was not a labor of love; it was a labor of resentment and deceitfulness. Her life was a lie. When you compliment someone like that, you heap coals of fire on her head. For this woman, a change of heart was a repentant prayer away.

"Being" Rather than Acting

In the privacy of your own heart, when no one is around, you need to be satisfied with yourself.

> **But the way of the unfaithful is hard.**
>
> PROV. 13:15

> **He who covers his sins will not prosper,**
> **But whoever confesses and forsakes them will have mercy.**
>
> PROV. 28:13

You may be clothed in the best of apparel, ride in the best of cars, and live in the best of homes, but you cannot cover your own sin. You must not only appear contented; you must also *be* contented. It is important that you be upright in heart and have a clear conscience.

A frightened mother tearfully told this story. She had two young children who were constantly fighting with each other. She was at a loss to know how to handle them. The strain of continuously unsuccessful efforts at controlling her children had exhausted her. Life to her was one frustration, day after day in a world of crying, squabbling, fighting children. One day, as she was peeling potatoes, she found herself thinking, "I could cut those kids up with this knife!" She was frightened at such thoughts and turned to a counselor for help.

She wanted the counselor to know that she loved her children with all her heart, that she would not hurt them for the world. To have thoughts of violence toward her children was a strange way of expressing her love, was it not? How far would a young man get if, when he was courting his girl, he would say, "I love you, but I feel like cutting you up with a knife. You annoy me. I cannot stand having you around!"?

The first step in finding the answer to this lady's problem was to help her recognize her lack of love. What is meant by *love*? I am not talking about hugs and kisses, or passion. You do not have to be married to find someone who can arouse passion within you. I am talking about the kind of love that is not your own. It is not developed through interaction between two people. It is not a tiny flame that is fanned into a blaze by two people being pleasant to each other. I am talking about a love that is consistent, independent of circumstances or of the behavior of the other—a love that comes from God. It is the Spirit of God that causes you to react to people and circumstances according to the fruit of the Spirit: love, joy, peace, long-suffering, gentleness, goodness, faith, meekness, and temperance.

If we are to receive the fruit of the Spirit, we must submit ourselves to God. This requires, first of all, willingness to treat people in a way that pleases God. Second, it requires submission to a power that is not your own. You alone are not capable of responding consistently to adverse treatment in a manner consistent with the fruit of the Spirit. As you submit to God, your inner response and your behavior toward others will reflect this power that is not your own.

The Bible breaks down the word *love* into its various parts:

Love is patient and kind; love never boils with jealousy; it never boasts, is never puffed with pride; it does not act with rudeness, or insist upon its rights; it never gets provoked, it never harbors evil thoughts, is never glad when wrong is done, but always glad when truth prevails.

1 COR. 13:4–6, WILLIAMS TRANSLATION

These are our inward characteristics. Your sense of well-being is based upon what goes on in your heart. Pastor, examine your heart moment by moment and

**Keep your heart with all diligence,
For out of it *spring* the issues of life**

PROV. 4:23

When the lady in this illustration began to recognize her "lack," she was on the road to a happy relationship with her children. She needed to be loving, not to act loving. This lady was basically dissatisfied with herself and her feelings of annoyance toward her children. Since she was not satisfied with herself, she could not be satisfied with her neighbors—her children.

THE PEACE OF A CLEAR CONSCIENCE

Several newspaper stories illustrate the importance of a clear conscience. A repentant forty-seven-year-old fugitive hitchhiked from Montana to Michigan on crutches to give himself up to police on a ten-year-old bad check charge. The fugitive had a seventeen-year-old son who enlisted recently in the Navy. The fugitive, crippled painfully by arthritis, was also wanted for breaking parole. He wanted to get a clean start in life, so he told the police and came back to face the consequences of his mistakes. He said he talked the matter over with his son before surrendering. "We thought if I had to return to prison I could serve my sentence and be out by the time my son got out of the Navy so we could be together. He's a fine boy, and I hope some day to earn his respect."

Is it not wonderful that this man came to the point where he was ready to confess and repent and start over? Just picture the day when the two men will be together again. It is never too late to repent, but this particular story had an unexpected ending. The police said that the warrant for the fugitive's arrest lapsed several years ago and that checks needed for evidence against him had been lost. The prosecutor agreed to dismiss the charges. Evidence was gone. No one could prove a thing. But the man had a conscience. He had to repent. He had to be forgiven.

Here is another illustration: Harry bought a dog for $10.00. About a year later the dog disappeared. He made every effort to find it, with no success. Just recently a car bearing a Nebraska license drove into their yard. The driver came to the house and said, "I am the fellow who took your dog many years ago. It has troubled me, and I want to pay for the animal." He paid Harry for a dog stolen nearly twenty-five years ago. That deceitful act pricked the man's conscience so much that he had to make that trip from Nebraska to confess personally. He had to do it.

The poet put it very well when he said,

> *There is a secret in his breast*
> *That will never let him rest.*

Here is another example that illustrates the truth that any act of unrighteousness can prick the conscience. It need not be a major crime. The driver of an M & S Pop truck one day found this note on the truck:

Dear Mr. M & S Pop Man:
   My brother and I are very sorry that we took the pop that was missing and we would like to pay you."

The driver opened the envelope and found two dimes.

The road to peace, contentment, and happiness is paved with truth, honesty, and integrity. You can fool your parents, your wife, your husband, and your congregation. These people can never know all the details of our lives. You can even fool yourself.

Good relations with your neighbor depend upon a good estimate of yourself. This is not pride or arrogance but a humble, warm realization that your practices can stand the scrutiny of God. Only then will you be a happy person. It is in this sense that you should love yourself.

A statement by Phillips Brooks gives a positive basis for happy living:

> To keep clear of concealment, to keep clear of the need of concealment, to do nothing which he might not do out on the middle of Boston Common at noon day—I cannot say how more and more that seems to me to be the glory of a young man's life. It is an awful hour when the first necessity of hiding anything comes. The whole life is different thenceforth. When there are questions to be feared and eyes to be avoided and subjects which must not be touched, then the bloom of life is gone. Put off that day as long as possible. Put it off forever if you can. Can your actions stand publicity?

Each of us at times sins. When we do, one of the most wholesome steps is to repent. Do so as fast as you know you have done something wrong. It seems that we have a little built-in justifier in our bodies. When we err and it gets a little warm, it kicks in like a thermostat and we start justifying ourselves. One of the easiest ways to start an argument is to start justifying ourselves. Just repent when you err—so that there is nothing to hide, nothing to justify.

None of us can dictate the circumstances in our lives. But the source of the Spirit is God, not people or circumstances of your life. You can determine your reactions to them. You can maintain a pure heart and a good conscience. You can avail yourself of the love of God that will enable you to love your neighbor.

> **My little children, let us not love in word or in tongue, but in deed and in truth. And by this we know that we are of the truth, and shall assure our hearts before Him. For if our heart condemns us, God is greater than our heart, and knows all things. Beloved, if our heart does not condemn us, we have confidence toward God. And whatever we ask we receive from Him, because we keep His commandments and do those things that are pleasing in His sight. And this is His commandment: that we should believe on the name of His Son Jesus Christ and love one another, as He gave us commandment. Now he who keeps His commandments abides in**

Him, and He in him. And by this we know that He abides in us, by the Spirit whom He has given us.

1 JOHN 3:18–24

HOW TO RESPOND WHEN TROUBLE COMES

Jesus said that in our lives we would experience trouble (John 16:33), but He also instructed us as to how we should respond:

> You have heard that it was said, "You shall love your neighbor and hate your enemy." But I say to you, love your enemies, bless those who curse you, do good to those who hate you, and pray for those who spitefully use you and persecute you, that you may be sons of your Father in heaven; for He makes His sun rise on the evil and on the good, and sends rain on the just and on the unjust. For if you love those who love you, what reward have you? Do not even the tax collectors do the same?

MATT. 5:43–46

Suppose there is a crooked farmer and a Christian farmer. The crooked farmer gets just as much rain as the Christian. Is this fair? Yes, it is fair. It does not matter whether the people you work with are friendly to you or unfriendly, does it? Your reaction to the fellow that is hard to live with should not be any different than your reaction to the fellow who is easy to live with. The Lord makes His sun to rise on the evil and on the good, and He makes it rain on the just and on the unjust. What difference does it make whether you have much rain or little rain? That is not a measure of your relationship to the Lord. Whether you are poor or rich is no measure of your relationship to the Lord.

Loving those who do good and those who do evil is the measure of your relationship to God.

Loving those who do good and those who do evil is the measure of your relationship to God. Then you will like what you see the next time you look yourself in the eye in the mirror. You have measured up to the standard all of us are to live by. I do believe that many of us are not consciously aware of why we are less than joyful. If we would get this principle in our minds, and become sensitive to God's standards, keep our sins confessed, and keep ourselves in the way of the power of God, we would find increasingly that the choices or behavior of other people will not bother us. We should be able to live joyously in any circumstances that confront us.

What a relief to walk in the Spirit. While life is calm, look at another example of handling trouble. Peter said,

> **For what credit is it if, when you are beaten for your faults, you take it patiently? But when you do good and suffer, if you take it patiently, this is commendable before God. For to this you were called, because Christ also suffered for us, leaving us an example, that you should follow His steps:**
>
> **"Who committed no sin,**
>
> **Nor was deceit found in His mouth";**
>
> **who, when He was reviled, did not revile in return; when He suffered, He did not threaten, but committed Himself to Him who judges righteously.**
>
> 1 PET. 2:20–23

Obviously, the one who walks in the Spirit will respond the way Jesus did. When you move away from quiet meditation into the consulting room, you are where the rubber meets the road. For example, a woman is sitting across from me who has been beaten up by her husband. She might still have some of the black and blue marks, and she shows them to me. She is furious, angry, and filled with hatred toward him. She wants me to approve of her reaction toward her husband. This becomes a test of my commitment to the Lord whom I love. He requires me to speak the truth in love. I need to love this lady and her husband. I need wisdom. How much truth do I share and when? She needs a change of heart. She needs to calm down. She needs some compassion toward her husband. Then she will be able to think straight. People do not like that.

She says, "I suppose if you were in my shoes, if someone beat you up, you would like it, huh?"

That depends on my spiritual condition at the time. Yes, I would respond the same way if I were a normal person. What would a spiritual response look like? How would Jesus handle it? He would protect her like He did the harlot taken in the act.

I must help her to look at her sins. Clearly she has anger and hatred. She needs to have a compassionate, forgiving spirit toward her assailant, even though his behavior is unacceptable. She must figure out a way to protect herself. At the same time she must consider if she has contributed to arousing the passions of the one who abused her. The good news is that the fruit of the Spirit is available to her immediately. She does not need to fix her environment before she can fix her heart. To respond this way to her husband without a change of heart is an impossibility.

I have seen missionaries on the mission field who could only see dirt, bugs, heat, and the danger of disease. Then there are other missionaries who are lost in the ministry to the people whom they love and they do not seem to notice these things. When there is someone doing something that is irritating, we are forced to admit that we do not love God with all our hearts and all our souls and all our minds. We are more concerned about ourselves—our comforts and well-being—rather than about this person who is irritating us. You need to love your neighbor. It does not have anything to do with his behavior. He is the recipient of your relationship to God—whatever it happens to be. When we talk about how you treat your neighbor, that is quite different than talking about loving your neighbor. How you treat your neighbor is observable. But loving your neighbor—that has to do with your Spirit. You can be very nice in behavior to a neighbor, but you may not love him.

> **Since you have purified your souls in obeying the truth through the Spirit in sincere love of the brethren, love one another fervently with a pure heart.**
>
> 1 PET. 1:22

This is the end of the commandment. This is the fruit that we are to display. Then at the end of the day we will be satisfied with our thoughts, feelings, words, and behavior. If not, we will repent, confessing our sins and praying to God for strength for tomorrow.

> **For the Chief Musician. A Psalm of David.**
> **O LORD, You have searched me and known me.**

You know my sitting down and my rising up;
You understand my thought afar off.
You comprehend my path and my lying down,
And are acquainted with all my ways.
For there is not a word on my tongue,
But behold, O LORD,
You know it altogether.
You have hedged me behind and before,
And laid Your hand upon me.
Such knowledge is too wonderful for me;
It is high, I cannot attain it.
Where can I go from Your Spirit?
Or where can I flee from Your presence?
If I ascend into heaven, You are there;
If I make my bed in hell,
behold, You are there.
If I take the wings of the morning,
And dwell in the uttermost parts of the sea,
Even there Your hand shall lead me,
And Your right hand shall hold me.
If I say, "Surely the darkness shall fall on me,"
Even the night shall be light about me;
Indeed, the darkness shall not hide from You,
But the night shines as the day;
The darkness and the light are both alike to You.

Ps. 139:1–12

HENRY T. BLACKABY

I see and speak with many pastors in "burnout" or "moral failure" or being "forced out of their pastorate." They and their families are unhappy, discontented, and unfulfilled. I often hear someone say, "But this is a terrible time to be a pastor. There are so many pressures, demands, and expectations on the pastor. It is no wonder they are angry, bitter, frustrated, disappointed, burned out, and unfulfilled."

This is a justification for acting unChristlike. In many instances, they are experiencing "fruit" of their own sin. It is not spiritual warfare, but the discipline of God. Their pressures, unhappiness, and lack of inner peace and contentment are often the result of sin, or the discipline of God. The ones the Lord loves He disciplines—even "scourges"—to produce holiness in His own (Heb. 12:3–7). The source of peace and contentment in ministry is *obedience* to God.

> **Therefore, whether you eat or drink, or whatever you do, do all to the glory of God. Give no offense, either to the Jews or to the Greeks or to the church of God.**
>
> 1 Cor. 10:31–33

Paul was instructing believers that in everything they do they should
1. Do it all to the glory of God. That is, set your heart not on self, but on God. Peace and joy and fulfillment come from a relationship with God, where the heart is set on bringing the greatest possible praise and affirmation and witness to God.
2. "Give no offense"—or, be blameless before others. Paul had stated that he was "free" to do anything. But not everything he was free to do would "edify" others. Some things he could do would indeed cause others "for whom Christ died" to stumble (Rom. 14:7–23; 1 Cor. 8:9–13; 10:23–24).

Paul lived fully for His Lord and also urged

> **And whatever you do in word or deed, do all in the name of the Lord Jesus, giving thanks to God the Father through Him.**
>
> Col. 3:17

> **And whatever you do, do it heartily, as to the Lord and not to men, knowing that from the Lord you will receive the reward of the inheritance; for you serve the Lord Christ.**
>
> Col. 3:23–24

Serving the Lord "heartily"—that is, with all the heart—is the true source of peace, joy, and fullness. Contentment is not determined by environment, circumstances, or the approval of others.

I faced this choice constantly. While pastoring a small, struggling church, seeking faithfully to start mission churches, and raise a family, there were those who heard about our sincere efforts and were modestly helping us in a much-needed financial way. Just when we were being relieved from financial pressure, a pastor sought to go to some of our contributors and undermine our ministry. He was successful in getting a major contributor to withdraw crucial support. Would that affect or remove peace and contentment? It did create the opportunity for me to choose to be offended, depressed, or discouraged. But it could not make me that way.

As best I knew we were doing all "as unto the Lord" and for His glory! So in the midst of this I turned to the Lord and cried out to Him. He, in return, gave me

- a great sense of His peace, and His affirmation;
- an assurance from Him of His provisions (which came and were fully adequate);
- an assurance that He would continue to give us peace and fulfillment—if, in everything, we would seek His glory.

The pain of a betrayal was real, but it did not *make* me discouraged or depressed. God Himself was my life! He was my peace! He was my fullness! Nothing outside me can affect my relationship to God. Absolute, joyful obedience to God ensured real peace in my heart.

Peace and fulfillment come from a sincere relationship with God, and our Lord Jesus Christ, who called us. Because of our calling, we, at all times, seek to please Him.

> **Therefore we make it our aim, whether present or absent, to be well pleasing to Him.**
>
> 2 COR. 5:9

We do all as unto our Lord and not unto other people. We live with our Lord in view. We look always to the "author and finisher of our faith" (Heb. 12:1–2). When our focus is on people and whether they follow us, respond favorably to us, affirm us, or recognize us with gifts and praise, we are courting pain and disappointment. Our peace in ministry comes from a strong and clear relationship with God. He gives the affirmation; He provides His love—and this is enough!

But how does a pastor keep in this relationship that brings him peace?

> **Keep your heart with all diligence,**
> **For out of it spring the issues of life.**
>
> PROV. 4:23

You have a choice. Guard your heart, the center of your life. Stand guard over your relationship with Christ. Keep Him close; talk with Him in prayer and in your time spent in His Word. Cultivate His loving presence deliberately while with others, in times alone, and even while preaching and teaching. Be preeminently aware of Him at all times. His love will keep your heart. A heart kept in the love of Christ will reveal itself in and during all other experiences in life.

The prophet Isaiah knew this:

> **You will keep him in perfect peace,**
> **Whose mind is stayed on You,**
> **Because he trusts in You.**
>
> ISA. 26:3

Jesus Himself is our peace:

> **"These things I have spoken to you, that in Me you may have peace. In the world you will have tribulation; but be of good cheer, I have overcome the world."**
>
> JOHN 16:33

Paul concurred:

> **For He Himself is our peace, who has made both one, and has broken down the middle wall of separation.**
>
> EPH. 2:14

The truth that can set us free, and keep us free, is what Paul described as the "fruit of the Spirit."

> **But the fruit of the Spirit is love, joy, peace. . . .**
>
> GAL. 5:22–23

When we walk in harmony with the Holy Spirit and in His power, He will bring love, joy, and peace into real experience. A pastor or leader must not only believe in his head all that the Holy Spirit *is*, and will do, but must "live according to the Spirit" (Rom. 8:5), and "walk in the Spirit" (Gal. 5:25), and "be led by the Spirit" (Rom. 8:14; Gal. 5:18).

God's wonderful provision for life at God's best is a life lived in, controlled by, and responsive to the Holy Spirit's presence and power. What we cannot do, He can and will do. No one can "make me angry"—when the Holy Spirit is controlling me. Nothing can disturb the peace of God in me when He is in control of me. But this relationship is a *choice* I make. I choose to release my life to His control. I then experience what Paul said about his life:

> **It is no longer I who live, but Christ lives in me; and the life which I now live in the flesh I live by faith in the Son of God, who loved me and gave Himself for me.**
>
> GAL. 2:20

Deliberately cultivating the life of the Son of God in me is crucial to peace and contentment in my life and ministry. When my life is lived with His peace, then I can lead others to experience His peace as well. I can bear witness to Him in my preaching and teaching and counseling, saying:

> **Be anxious for nothing, but in everything by prayer and supplication, with thanksgiving, let your requests be made known to God; and the peace of God, which surpasses all understanding, will guard your hearts and minds through Christ Jesus.**
>
> PHIL. 4:6–7

I remember so well the Lord directing me to visit fellow pastors every Friday. I would ask the Lord about whom I should visit. I knew clearly, one Friday, I should visit a neighboring pastor of another denomination. When I arrived at his office, his eyes were red—obviously from much weeping. He fell on my shoulder and gladly welcomed me as "a gift of God" to his life at that moment.

Then the story unfolded. He had been a successful businessman. He had responded to God's call to pastor in his late thirties. This was his first church. The previous night had been unusually and unbearably painful. The deacons had treated him harshly and spitefully. On returning home late and devastated, his wife said, "Our teenage son has just run away from home."

This man was hurting, broken, deeply depressed, and grieving. We turned to God's Word and read extensively, sharing as we read. He gradually and carefully turned his eyes and heart to his Lord. He had sought to bring glory to God and to faithfully please Him, but circumstances had taken a different turn. God, however, had remained the same. Together, on our knees, we turned our hearts to the Lord—and He heard our cry and gave His peace and assurance.

I then pledged my help—from our deacons to his, from our teenagers to his son, and our lives to his need. Over time, God heard and was pleased and honored. This pastor remained in the ministry (and is to this day). He, his church, and his son were restored!

By turning to God whom we love, believe, hear, and obey, His peace will guard our hearts and minds in Christ. This relationship is for every pastor and every leader. It is a choice—but it is a real choice—with God's full assurance of His faithfulness to His Word.

PROCESS THE MESSAGE

1. If it is your intent to love God as Jesus said you should, how would you go about it?

2. Can your actions stand publicity?

3. How would you know if you responded as a spiritual Christian?

4. Are there currently any circumstances in life that you are blaming for a lack of peace?

5. How do you respond to "difficult" people in the congregation?

NINE

God's Sufficiency—
The Sum and Substance
of Ministry

> *And we have such trust through Christ toward God. Not that we are sufficient of ourselves to think of anything as being from ourselves, but our sufficiency is from God, who also made us sufficient as ministers of the new covenant, not of the letter but of the Spirit; for the letter kills, but the Spirit gives life.*
>
> 2 CORINTHIANS 3:4–6
>
> *You have the capacity to develop your acting ability, maintain it, and improve it. We are not talking about acting here, we are talking about being yielded, letting God work in your life.*
>
> HENRY BRANDT
>
> *To fail to remain in fellowship with God and draw upon and receive from Him His life for our life, is to "receive the grace of God in vain."*
>
> HENRY T. BLACKABY

HENRY BRANDT

But the fruit of the Spirit is love, joy, peace, longsuffering, kindness, goodness, faithfulness, gentleness, self-control. Against such there is no law.

GAL. 5:22–23

These are our resources from God. I want to remind you that the fruit of the Spirit of God involves a relationship between you and Him. Circumstances and people will reveal your spirit, not determine your spirit.

Facing the Truth of God's Word

I will be eternally grateful for being placed in a job supervised by a mean, cussing, impolite boss. I hated him so much that it affected my work, my personal life, and my family life. He forced me into searching the Bible for an answer. I did not like what I found:

> **Let all bitterness, wrath, anger, clamor, and evil speaking be**
> **put away from you, with all malice.**
> **EPH. 4:31**

I was experiencing all of those. The twelve persons in my work group all agreed that our reactions toward the boss were reasonable behavior. When it comes right down to it, it is surprising how many people would rather be mad than glad. The next verse was worse yet:

> **And be kind to one another, tenderhearted, forgiving one**
> **another, just as God in Christ forgave you.**
> **EPH. 4:32**

Imagine being kind and tenderhearted and forgiving toward him. If I would have known where to go to get a spirit of kindness toward him, I would not have gone there. I was perfectly happy to be miserable. I did not want to be kind, compassionate and forgiving in spite of a clear biblical directive.

Anybody with any sense at all (the psychiatric and psychological literature all agree at least on this) would know that wrath, anger, malice, and bitterness are the cause of all kinds of aches, pains, and miseries.

If we agree on one thing in this world, we agree that there ought to be more kindness, more forgiveness, and more tenderness. We agree that there ought to be, but that is much different than wanting to be nice to that person who is rude to you.

Helplessness

I struggled with this for several months. I wanted to brush it aside, but I could not. Finally, one day I decided that God's Word was right. How about that! I would love my boss. If I made up my mind to do it, I could do it—or so I thought. I remember going to work having decided I would love him, but when he growled, "Brandt, come here!" I was as mad as ever. I found out that there are some things that you cannot *decide* to do, and that was one of them. I became madder yet at the Bible! God told me to do things I could not do. I did not realize the Bible also said I could not do it on my own. I kept searching the Scriptures and found an answer. This insight changed my outlook on life and even my profession. However, my first reaction to this verse was resistance. I did not even finish the verse; instead, I took offense to it.

> **Not that we are sufficient of ourselves to think of anything as being from ourselves, but our sufficiency is from God.**
>
> 2 COR. 3:5

I am sufficient. I got my education without God's help. I got my job without God's help. I got promotions without His help. I began accumulating some wealth. I did not need God for that—I thought!

I can live up to the etiquette book without God's help. I can get up off my chair with a smile on my face, and nobody will know there is hatred in my heart—the cesspool underneath my skin. You have the capability of improving your acting ability. Anybody who sets the objective of acting more like a Christian a year from now can reach that goal. You will not be any closer to being one, but you will sound like one. You will also look like one. We all can act.

I read the verse again when I finished telling myself how sufficient I was. It became clear that in reacting to a part of the verse I lost the message. Read the entire passage:

> **And we have such trust through Christ toward God. Not that we are sufficient of ourselves to think of anything as being from ourselves, but our sufficiency is from God, who also made us sufficient as ministers of the new covenant, not of the letter but of the Spirit; for the letter kills, but the Spirit gives life.**
>
> 2 COR. 3:4–6

All of us have the capacity to live up to the letter of the law. We can improve our performance. We can follow instructions and obey rules. In my case, I could approach my boss with a smile on my face. I could act with grace and do what he told me. I could improve my skills and add to my knowledge.

Finally I got it through my head that my inner life was what I could not manage. My aching abdomen was caused by holding in and covering up hatred, anger, bitterness, stubbornness, and rebellion. I cannot match an appropriate inner response with proper outer behavior.

For the letter kills, but the Spirit gives life.

2 COR. 3:6

An appropriate inner response is the difference between self-control and yielding to a new source of help. One word—"Brandt!"—changed me from being relaxed to a bundle of tension. I was helpless to stop my reaction. A helpless, screaming baby who cannot talk can trigger an adult to become so furious that the child is in danger.

I do not understand why we cling to sinful reactions to people and circumstances. Nor do I understand why we cease the struggle. I do know that I became convinced that I was helpless when my boss yelled at me. One word—"Brandt!"—triggered a massive hostile response. The best I could do was to manage this unwelcome reaction. It was killing me. One day, on the way to work I admitted my helplessness. I could not respond in a kindly, compassionate, forgiving way. I could not prevent a hostile response. I poured it all out to God. I needed His help. That day I watched my boss scan the room and yell, "Brandt, come here!" I responded willingly. For the first time I was not rebellious or angry. I was nice to him. I did not have to act nice. Would this freedom last?

Ministry of the Spirit

A week went by. Two weeks. Then one day I experienced the same old hostile, rebellious response. I learned a lesson. I had drifted away from a conscious, deliberate, dependence on the Lord. I was back to living up to the letter of the law. That choice remains to this day. It involves daily, life-long submission to the Spirit. That truth can come alive. Pastor, we have a ministry of the Spirit!—something invisible, something intangible, something that you cannot touch.

But the fruit of the Spirit is love, joy, peace, longsuffering, kindness, goodness, faithfulness, gentleness, self-control. Against such there is no law.

GAL. 5:22–23

An Act of the Will

I watched a Detroit Edison employee hook up a stove in one of our new restaurants. He said that when he completed the hookup I would be able to command the gas to flow from Texas to this stove. I could stop the flow or control the quantity of gas by simply moving a knob to the right or left.

In the same way we have access to God's resources. We can cut them off by an act of the will. The work of the Holy Spirit is available anytime. There is no person in the world who can interfere with it, and there is no situation that can cut you off from Him. However, you can turn away from the Spirit of God any time you want to, like you turn off the light in your room and plunge it into darkness. You did not disconnect yourself from the Source of power, but you did plunge into darkness.

> *In the privacy of your own heart, when no one is around, are you satisfied with yourself?*

You can stumble around in life, as if you never heard of God. You have the capability of doing the most devilish things if you want to. You do not need to, but you can. Part of God's plan is to allow you to choose if you will walk in the Spirit. There is an act of the will involved.

You have the capacity to develop your acting ability, maintain it, and improve it. We are not talking about acting here, we are talking about being yielded, letting God work in your life.

I cannot create heat or electricity, but I can draw upon the resources of the Detroit Edison Company. I cannot generate love, peace, or joy, but I can draw on an infinite supply. So can you.

> **[Jesus] also made us sufficient as ministers of the new covenant, not of the letter but of the Spirit; for the letter kills, but the Spirit gives life.**
>
> 2 COR. 3:6

I was a speaker for a spiritual life conference. A couple, who were mad at each other, asked me if I would talk to them. I had been talking about the ministry of the Spirit every night—all day Tuesday, all day Wednesday, and here it was Thursday—and these people were *still* mad at each other!

The wife was working hard at church, and ignoring the fact that her husband did not like it. She said, "You cannot interfere with my ministry to the Lord."

I said to this couple, "All week long we have been talking about the ministry of the Spirit, and look at you. You know what you need to do." I left.

These people finally did agree—they were both mad at *me*. Later this same lady slipped me a note: "We talked to you about a half hour ago and you walked out on us. I just want you to know the last half hour I have been sitting in my car. I got myself straightened out with God. Thank you."

We can listen to instruction and ignore it. It is like the fellow sitting in front of a piece of apple pie a la mode with a fork in his hand saying, "I should not eat this." He then proceeds to eat it. Knowing exactly what he is doing wrong, he can do wrong perfectly and consciously.

God is the only one who can change your spirit.

Ours is the ministry of the Spirit. Consider this Scripture:

> **But we have renounced the hidden things of shame, not walking in craftiness nor handling the word of God deceitfully, but by manifestation of the truth commending ourselves to every man's conscience in the sight of God. But even if our gospel is veiled, it is veiled to those who are perishing.**
>
> 2 COR. 4:2–3

Look at that verse in detail:

- Paul renounced secret and shameful ways.
- He was not deceptive.
- He loved the Bible.
- He set forth the truth plainly.
- He commended himself to a man's conscience in the sight of God.

Personal Deception

We can be deceptive with the best intentions. In fact, we can make the truth seem like the wrong, even destructive, way to go.

For example, our psychologists will tell us that it is very important to praise people, and I agree. People are entitled to realistic praise. We ought to let people know that we appreciate what they do, but, whether or not this praise benefits the person involved will depend upon whether that person deserves that praise. Somebody who comes up to you and praises your sacrificial deed that you did reluctantly is heaping coals of fire on your head. Praise, undeserved, can cause distress in the person receiving it. You might be causing a person to go home and weep bitter tears because they did not deserve your praise, and they know it.

Loving with God's Love

A friend of mine asked me, "What do you do when you do not want someone to keep coming over to your house? What do you tell him?"

"How do you treat him when he comes over?" I asked.

"I say, 'Hello, glad to see you, come on in.' We visit back and forth, and then he says, 'Maybe it's time for me to go.' Then I say, 'Oh no, sit down, sit down, you don't have to go yet.' So he sits down, we talk another half hour, and then maybe I will offer him a little refreshment. When he finally does go, I say, 'Glad you came, come again, won't you?'"

To say the least, my friend is misleading his guest. In the first place, as Christians we ought to like all people. If God's love is in our hearts, it will not make much difference who comes over.

> *Praise, undeserved, can cause distress in the person receiving it.*

Some people say, "But there are personality differences. You naturally respond to some people more than others." I say, yes, you do—naturally, but not spiritually.

How can you love everybody? It takes a miracle. Would it not be a tragedy if someone came to the Lord and He would not respond? Would it not be a tragedy if we took God up on His statement—"Come to Me all you who labor and are heavy laden, and I will give you rest"—and the Lord would not accept us?

If we try to keep God's commandments, we will quickly discover that this is a human impossibility. We must be born again, transformed, and walk in a Spirit that is not our own. This involves a lifetime of daily surrender to the Spirit of God.

All the people mentioned in this chapter needed some teaching about maintaining the spiritual side of life. They need to find a church equipped to help them. The result is worth the effort:

That we should no longer be children, tossed to and fro and carried about with every wind of doctrine, by the trickery of men, in the cunning craftiness of deceitful plotting, but, speaking the truth in love, may grow up in all things into Him who is the head—Christ.

EPH. 4:14–15

Honesty

What is the difference between honest people and dishonest people? A dishonest person *looks* like an honest one. You cannot detect any physical difference. Dishonesty is invisible. Very few people would consider themselves to be deceitful schemers, however.

You pay a great price when you depart from truth, integrity, honesty, and when you start blaming someone else for your unhappiness. Relationships taper off over a period of months and months, not overnight. There may be a crisis, but that will only bring to a head that which has been coming for a long, long time.

> *To love your neighbor is not to subtly set the stage for getting what you want, but to help meet your neighbor's needs.*

To love your neighbor is not to subtly set the stage for getting what you want, but to help meet your neighbor's needs.

Counterfeits can look pretty good. I recall my experience going into a house and seeing a dish of pears. They made my mouth water. I said to my son, "I am going to get me one of those pears." When I got close, I saw they were wax. They were counterfeit, and I was disappointed. They looked like pears, were shaped like pears, had the color of pears; but they were not pears. We want to be sure that our service to people is not like that, don't we? Our charity should be backed by a pure heart and a good conscience and sincere faith. When the going gets tough, we will be an effective witness for Christ.

To manipulate people and force them to do what you want them to do without them knowing you are behind it is, to say the least, dishonest.

Occasionally someone will call me and say, "Doc, I have a friend who needs some help, but he won't go for any help. I would like to give a dinner party and invite my friend so that the two of you can sit together." It will come out sometime during the evening that I am a psychologist— and I am supposed to act like it is just a coincidence.

A man called to tell me he had some helpful information about his friend who was my client. I have learned to say that I will be glad to listen, provided I can quote him. Consequently, the man did not give me the information. The question is not should we speak the truth. The question is what is the best way to do it.

We become so concerned whether interaction with somebody goes smoothly, that we will go to great lengths to avoid conflict. We will lie, deceive, mislead, just to avoid upsetting anybody. Many times individuals will leave counseling sessions all upset because I told them the truth. People eventually get over being upset. They think about what you said. I have come to depend upon a second reaction, and not the first.

I commend myself unto your conscience, not your behavior. If we want to have effective ministries, this is what we will do.

HENRY T. BLACKABY

I have always trembled at the biblical qualifications of a pastor (bishop) given in 1 Timothy 3:1–7 and Titus 1:5–16. What especially overwhelmed me were the qualifications of a bishop in Titus 1:6–9:

- blameless
- a steward of God
- not self-willed
- not quick tempered
- a lover of what is good, sober-minded, just, holy, self-controlled
- holding fast the faithful word

1 Timothy 3:2–7 adds:

- not greedy for money
- gentle, not quarrelsome
- having a good testimony among those who are outside

Each of the statements was clear, certain, and mandatory. In addition were the "fruit of the Spirit," which, if I were to teach, I must model in my own life: love, joy, peace, longsuffering, kindness, goodness, faithfulness, gentleness, and self-control. Then God added, by way of reminder, what *agape* love was:

> **Love suffers long and is kind; love does not envy; love does not parade itself, is not puffed up; does not behave rudely, does not seek its own, is not provoked, thinks no evil; does not rejoice in iniquity, but rejoices in the truth; bears all things, believes all things, hopes all things, endures all things. Love never fails. But whether there are prophecies, they will fail; whether there are tongues, they will cease; whether there is knowledge, it will vanish away.**
>
> 1 COR. 13:4–8

Too good to be true? No! These words were God's guidelines for my life. But how is such a life possible, in our world, especially since God did not give these character qualities as a suggestion but as a command? This picture of a faithful pastor is only possible through the presence of Christ and the mighty resources of God's fullness and grace in our life.

Everything a pastor or leader needs for victorious living and ministry is already provided, and always immediately available to all who choose to receive them, and by faith live in the victory of them.

GOD'S SUFFICIENCY—THE SUM AND SUBSTANCE OF OUR MINISTRY

I looked in the Bible at God's expectations and His absolute character qualities necessary for a servant of God whom He can use and whose life will honor Him: Ephesians 1:17–23; 3:14–21; Colossians 2:9–10; 2 Corinthians 1:20; 9:8; 2 Peter 1:2–11. I was overwhelmed! But, "walking in the Spirit" means that at every command the Holy Spirit reveals, or impresses in His servant how to respond. He will also immediately reveal God's wonderful resources. The Scriptures listed above were brought to my mind and my heart! But God who showed me His expectations also showed me His provisions:

- His full resurrection power in the Scripture (Eph. 1:17–23) and in the churches I would serve

- His own fullness (Eph. 3:20)
- His own enabling, implemented by His own power (Eph. 3:21) and done in the churches I would serve
- Every promise God had ever given was automatically "Yes!" in Christ (2 Cor. 1:20)
- All grace abounding toward me—at all times, in all circumstances, in all things, and for every good work (2 Cor. 9:8)

Every promise God had ever given? Yes! Had I ever listed them? Had I ever asked Him to enable me to hear, understand, and do them in my life? Was I living below my inheritance? I was an heir and joint heir with Christ (Rom. 8:16–17). Had I been living all the practical areas of my life and ministry in the reality of all God had made available? The answer was a humbling "No."

I asked God to forgive me and help me live daily in the light of His Word and His promises. I asked the Holy Spirit to teach me (John 14:26) and guide me "into all truth" (John 16:13). And I asked my Lord Jesus to live out His life in me as He had lived in the Father. The response to my choice to trust Him was a resounding "Yes!" I turned to Him in my marriage, my family, and in the church I was guiding. I turned to Him for finances, and He heard and provided in wonderful and personal ways for our family, our church, and our missions. He was never late or short, and my wife would add, "never early."

I asked Him for His wisdom in key decisions, and I guided our church to seek His wisdom in faith. Each time God touched our minds, hearts, and wills, it was special and fresh and new—not a method but an intimate relationship with Him.

I asked for courage and boldness, and it was granted—especially when what we knew God asked us to do was not accepted by others. This was so true at a meeting where many churches came together. I took some students with me, for we had made a request from this group of churches to find it in their hearts to help us financially, even in a modest way. We were carrying a very heavy load all alone. But some strongly opposed the request. Our students wept in disbelief! I took them aside and pointed out a few things:

- God Himself had promised to be our supply.
- We had made this request sincerely.

- His people at this time were saying, "No!"
- We would continue to trust the Lord—and not allow this moment to be seen as rejection by men but as a new direction by God.

We prayed in joyful submission and obedience. Our hearts remained fixed on God's adequate and timely supply. For ten more years He met our every need. I moved away, and we no longer gave direction to the Bible college that was developed. But we all came to experience God's sufficiency as the essence of our ministry.

Moses gave this same assurance to God's people in Deuteronomy 30:11–20. He concluded by reminding them it was a choice they had to make:

> **I have set before you life and death, blessing and cursing; therefore choose life, that both you and your descendants may live; that you may love the LORD your God, that you may obey His voice, and that you may cling to Him, for He is your life.**
>
> DEUT. 30:19–20

What an assurance is now available to all who believe God and receive His presence as our provision for all things and in all things and at all times! The assignment is overwhelming, but God's resources are more than adequate for every occasion. The key is our relationship with God. Nothing has greater significance than this, and nothing determines more thoroughly the shape and outcome of our ministry!

I have spent hundreds of hours with pastors and leaders who expressed discouragement, frustration, and disappointment. Not one have I encountered who could not have faced each situation with God and seen and experienced victory. It is impossible to stand fully in the presence of God, and remain there for any length of time in fellowship with Him and His Son (1 John 1:3–4) and His Spirit (2 Cor. 13:14) and be discouraged! He is your life (Deut. 30:19–20; John 14:6). When you turn to Him, He reveals that

- When you are weak—He is strong (2 Cor. 12:9–10).
- When you do not know what to pray—He will help you (Rom. 8:26).
- No matter what, He will work all things together for good (Rom. 8:28).

- Where sin abounds, grace does much more abound (Rom. 5:20–21).
- Nothing can separate you from His love (Rom. 8:37–39).
- All authority is His (Matt. 28:18).
- What is humanly impossible is possible with God (Matt. 19:26).
- You are filled with all God's fullness (Eph. 3:19).
- All things are under Christ's feet (Eph. 1:22–23).
- God never leaves us or forsakes us (Heb. 13:5).
- God is faithful in every testing (1 Cor. 10:13).
- God never changes (Mal. 3:6).
- All God's wisdom and knowledge are yours (Col. 2:2–3).
- In faith, nothing will be impossible for you (Matt. 17:20).
- Every promise God has ever given is "Yes!" in Christ (2 Cor. 1:20).
- God always causes us to triumph (2 Cor. 2:14).

And countless other truth is always ours, by faith and in life. Jesus said, "You shall know [experience] the truth, and the truth shall make you free" (John 8:31–32, 36).

Many times I have stood before God and remained in His presence until He became to me, by faith, all He has always revealed. Never has God been unfaithful when I trusted Him. He is faithful in financial need, in need for laborers, in need for guidance, or strength, or wisdom, or discernment, or courage, in needs in my personal life, my family, or my ministry.

With five precious children and, at the time, living on next to nothing as a pastor in pioneer missions, we wondered (aloud), "How will we ever get each of these children through braces, college, and/or seminary?" God gave us, through my wife, the immediate and wonderful assurance: "I will never leave you, nor forsake you!"

The years had to pass—and they now have—and God, whom we trusted and obeyed, out of "His riches" has taken all five children through university and seminary—debt free! Each one was different, but all were assured! In every aspect of life and ministry, God's sufficiency is our very life. (Read carefully Deut. 30:19–20; 2 Pet. 1:2–11.)

David realized this fully:

> **Blessed is the man**
> **Who walks not in the counsel of the ungodly,**
> **Nor stands in the path of sinners,**

Nor sits in the seat of the scornful;
But his delight is in the law of the LORD,
And in His law he meditates day and night.
He shall be like a tree
Planted by the rivers of water,
That brings forth its fruit in its season,
Whose leaf also shall not wither;
And whatever he does shall prosper.

PS. 1:1–3

To fail to remain in fellowship with God and draw upon and receive from Him His life for our life, is to "receive the grace of God in vain" (2 Cor. 6:1) and be dependent on our own resources (so pitiful in the presence of His) and the resources and counsel of others (nothing compared to His).

A servant of the Lord must strain every fiber of his being to remain "in Christ" and His life, for Jesus said,

> **I am the vine, you are the branches. He who abides in Me, and I in him, bears much fruit; for without Me you can do nothing.**

JOHN 15:5

To remain "in His love," is to experience the fullness of Christ's joy! (John 15:9–11).

Every day I make it a habit to get up early and spend time with God in His Word and in prayer. I began to sense I was being hurried in my time with God because of the pressure of the day's agenda. Then the Spirit began to "guide me into all truth" and reminded me that my time with God must not be rushed. Why? For He is my life.

> **"That you may love the LORD your God, that you may obey His voice, and that you may cling to Him, for He is your life and the length of your days."**

DEUT. 30:20

To hurry Him was to shortchange everything else. I began to get up earlier so that I could spend tranquil time with Him. Each time I would feel rushed, I began a little earlier. This is still my goal: *I will not be hurried or pressured in the presence of God! He is God!* More can happen in me in His Presence than anything else I do! I will not hurry Him!

What an incredible difference time with God has made and continues to make in my life. I would not "exchange" this time alone and unhurried before God for anything in the world. God has my full attention as long as He wants, when I meet Him.

I have learned three things from Jeremiah 29:11–14:

1. God's thoughts and purposes toward me are good.
2. He has such hope and a future for me.
3. When I come to Him, when I call on Him, when I seek Him with all my heart, He always listens and hears and is experientially present and active to lead me and enable me to His best.

In my fellowship with God, He has kept His fullness in my life personally, in my marriage, in my family, and in my ministry.

PROCESS THE MESSAGE

---

1. Is there an area of your life that you need to pour out to God and say to Him that you need His help? If so, take time now to respond to Him.

2. In the privacy of your own heart, when no one is around, are you satisfied with yourself?

3. Are there any people you work or serve with whom you have difficulty loving? What does that show you about your heart?

4. You pay a great price when you depart from truth, integrity, and honesty, and when your conscience begins to prick you and you start blaming someone else for your unhappiness. Can you remember a situation when you or a close friend paid a great price? What did it cost?

5. God's resources are more than adequate for every occasion. How would your family or friends recognize this was true in your life?

TEN

God—The Supplier
of All Your Needs

> *Rejoice always, pray without ceasing, in everything give*
> *thanks; for this is the will of God in Christ Jesus for you.*
> 1 THESSALONIANS 5:16–18
>
> *There is a spirit of faith available every day independent*
> *of circumstances, independent of people, and of people's*
> *choices. On any given day, you have an option. You can*
> *submit your life to the Lord, but you do not have to. You*
> *can rejoice, but you do not have to. That leaves you with a*
> *daily choice. Which way will you choose?*
> HENRY BRANDT
>
> *God led me to realize that He was God and I wasn't! I seek*
> *to always remember that, especially when I am in His*
> *presence and in difficult circumstances.*
> HENRY T. BLACKABY

HENRY BRANDT

This thought occurred to me one day as the jet shot into the air from the runway at Los Angeles Airport. Out of my window was a glimpse of the Pacific Ocean with its sandy beaches. In a few minutes it disappeared as the plane entered a cloud. Later at 35,000 feet, we got a glimpse of the Grand Canyon. It looked like a snapshot. Panoramas from a plane can be vast, breathtaking, brief, and gone.

Rules for effective living pass in the same way. Basic, crucial laws are sometimes mentioned as wispy afterthoughts. It does not seem very profound to say, "Good health depends in part on a balanced diet and exercise." Those eleven words sum up a principle that involves study, experience, discipline, industry and labor, money, and daily attention. To ignore the rule opens the door to much sickness.

In Bible study, you can flit past a rule for living like a quick glimpse of the Grand Canyon from a jet moving at 500 miles per hour.

Pastor, nine words can change your life and the lives of your people. To ignore them opens the door to years of misery. All the benefits of health, education, and wealth can be enjoyed either by accepting them or neutralized by ignoring them. To reap the benefits requires a lifetime of attention, sacrifice, and cooperation.

Look at these nine words:

Rejoice always, pray without ceasing, in everything give thanks.
1 THESS. 5:16–18

JOY

Rejoice always. (v. 16)

It is not very long; it is not very complicated. It is only two words: *rejoice always*. All the time? Think that one over. You wonder whether this writer understood about modern-day pressures. Did he know what teenagers are like, what wives and husbands can do to each other? Did he understand some of today's business pressures? And we are supposed to rejoice all the time?

I was flying out of Atlanta one afternoon and had left early to get to the airport in plenty of time. I sat outside the terminal with the person who drove me, and we chatted for about fifteen minutes. Soon after the conversation I entered the airport and handed the attendant my boarding pass. She said, "Sir, that plane left."

I looked at my watch; I had fifteen minutes to spare. Her clock was running, and mine had stopped. Instead of being on my way to Asheville, North Carolina, I would spend the night in a hotel in Atlanta.

When I realized I could not get to Asheville, I hastened to a phone to call the director of the conference center where I was to speak. You see, he was now without a speaker. The fellow who had to drive fifty miles to the airport to meet me had already left. Both these men needed some joy to finish the day.

I realized that I had two options: I could enjoy the evening by submitting to the joy of the Lord, or I could fuss and cuss and get mad at God because I failed to pay attention to my watch.

To enjoy such events is a human impossibility. It takes a miracle. I did enjoy that evening. The next morning I got up at 5:30 and was first in line to board the plane bound for Asheville. I asked the Lord to help me practice this verse, "Rejoice always." Forty-five minutes later as the plane was flying around Asheville, I sensed something was wrong because I felt the airplane climbing. The pilot announced there was fog in Asheville and that we would make one more attempt. If we did not succeed, we would go to Johnson City, Tennessee—the gateway to the beautiful Smoky Mountains. You should have seen the mood change in that airplane. Everybody began to grumble and get mad because there was fog in Asheville.

Your peace of mind should not depend on whether there is fog in Asheville. I just asked the Lord to help me enjoy this day. Once we landed in Johnson City, this planeload of irate, well-dressed people descended on a poor, unsuspecting young man behind the counter at the airport.

One passenger put it this way, "We demand to get to Asheville!" The poor fellow behind the counter did not cause the fog in Asheville. I was meditating on my verses. I felt sorry for him, so I went to him and told him that I, too, just got off this plane, but I was one person he did not have to worry about. I told him I would wait and when he got through with the rest of them, he could take care of me. I offered him my moral support. When you think about it, there was nothing anyone could do about it—not a thing.

I soon called the conference director to let him know that he did not have a speaker that morning. He said the same fellow who drove to the airport last night to pick me up had already left this morning. They needed a source of joy that day.

Finally, the airlines provided three old Volkswagen buses. The people started piling into those buses—miserable-looking people, packed in like sardines, starting up the drive to see the Smokies.

Then the fellow called me over and said, "I am sorry, sir, but we have no more room. I tell you what, we have a Chrysler limousine over here. I will send you in that limousine." I accepted his offer.

Maybe I was not as spiritual as I could have been as we passed those Volkswagens. One's spiritual life is not determined by the type of transportation that is available, is it? The director of the conference had planned this a year ago. Yet there was fog in Asheville, and I could not get there. I wonder what God had in mind for the conference director and me to learn?

PRAYER

Pray without ceasing.

1 THESS. 5:17

You cannot do that. I am not praying right now. Neither are you. All kinds of activities that we must perform keep us from praying. What does the verse mean? I believe it means that we should have a prayerful attitude. We do not need to worry about how things turn out. Who cares if there is fog in Asheville this morning anyway? I do not think I need to be anxious about that. I can do what I can do as though everything depended on me, but God can overrule.

> *I can do what I can do as though everything depended on me, but God can overrule.*

I was in an airport (again) and the thought just popped in my head, *I should call Mike*. So I did.

Mike's wife answered. She said, "Oh, am I glad you called, I was praying you would call. Something terrible has happened. Mike has lost his business."

I talked to Mike, and sure enough he had lost a multimillion-dollar business. It was not all his fault. He was the victim of some other people's choices, but he had lost his business anyway. I was on my way out of town, but I made an appointment to meet him at one of our restaurants later. (I owned restaurants at the time.) I did not realize what I was doing. This was a booming, busy place and there was always a line of people waiting to get in. So I invite this fellow who lost his business to come and meet me at my business which is just booming. Six years before, Mike and I agreed that the two of us would go into business. One of the reasons was so that we would be free to serve the Lord and contribute some of our funds to the Lord's work.

I asked Mike, "What have you been doing with your time?" All he did for six years was pour himself into that business.

"What have you done with your money?" He invested in the business, expanding more and more.

"What have you given to the Lord's work?"

Mike said, "I have been investing it in the business. Maybe next year we can put some in the Lord's work."

So you see what happened. He did not keep his word. He was no good to the Lord, time wise or money wise. What could I say? I remembered that Bible verse: "Pray without ceasing." All I could think of was, *If I were a loving heavenly father I would have taken your business away from you because you were designing a millstone around your neck. It seems to me that because God cares about you, He removed something that is not good for you to have.*

If you promised God that you would give Him some of your time and money, and you were not doing it, I think God would do what is best for you. If you committed your works to the Lord, you could trust that it would turn out in your best interests. It seems to me that "praying continually" is committing what you have to the Lord and trusting Him. You do not need to worry about how it turns out.

You wonder, did the apostle Paul know what he was talking about when he wrote that? Isn't this is the potential of the Christian life? This is why we are being motivated to tell people about Jesus. He is the pathway to rejoicing and relaxation. He is the One who allows us to go through this world comfortable and at ease and enjoying it. What do you think?

> *It seems to me that "praying continually" is committing what you have to the Lord and trusting Him.*

THANKFULNESS

In everything give thanks.

1 THESS. 5:18

Four words. In everything? Yes, in everything. The Bible says this is the will of God concerning you—to be thankful all the time.

Giving Thanks in Times of Sorrow

I remember getting together with Al and his wife at dinner one Saturday night. The next Saturday night, my wife and I were in a funeral home because Al's wife was in a coffin. This is one of the first times that anybody truly close to us died.

Al came running to me, looking distraught, disgusted, and frustrated. He said with such pleading eyes, "Henry, tell me something I need to hear."

I had the time that it takes to walk from the coffin to a couch to figure out what to tell him. I needed to pray! The question is did God have anything to say to him in this difficult time, using me as a channel?

I thought of a passage of Scripture, but I said to myself, *I cannot read that to him.* This man was upset and deeply troubled. Anyway, I forced myself to read it.

> **Grace to you and peace from God our Father and the Lord Jesus Christ.**
>
> 2 COR. 1:2

Who wants peace at a time like this? Society dictates that you should be unhappy and miserable. What do you do with a verse that says "rejoice always" now? What do you do with a verse that says "in everything give thanks" now? Or "pray without ceasing?" Do you conclude that these verses do not apply in a situation so full of grief as death? What do you say when your friend reaches out an empty hand and says, "Help me"?

> **Blessed be the God and Father of our Lord Jesus Christ, the Father of mercies and God of all comfort, who comforts us in all our tribulation, that we may be able to comfort those who are in any trouble, with the comfort with which we ourselves are comforted by God.**
>
> 2 COR. 1:3–4

I said to Al, "Now is the time for you to decide if the Bible means anything to you or not. If you could be comforted, would you want to be?"

"I do not know," Al stated.

When the pastor stood up to speak, he said, "I never had this happen before, but Al wants to give the message."

Al said, "As I stood by the coffin and watched the people pass by, everybody looked so hopeless and desperate. But I want to tell you that I have found the source of comfort. I just want to remind you at an occasion like this God will comfort you. But only one person reminded me of God's comfort."

Well, that was a shocker to me. I was uneasy and uncomfortable about reading him the very message that he should have heard. Imagine being uncomfortable about sharing God's Word! I want to share with you what Al read to the people at his wife's funeral:

> **As you have therefore received Christ Jesus the Lord, so walk in Him, rooted and built up in Him and established in the faith, as you have been taught, abounding in it with thanksgiving. Beware lest anyone cheat you through philosophy and empty deceit, according to the tradition of men, according to the basic principles of the world, and not according to Christ. For in Him dwells all the fullness of the Godhead bodily.**
>
> COL. 2:6–9

Al said, "The traditions of men would require me to be distraught and unhappy and miserable. Person after person went by and said, 'Al, you are doing all right now, but look out when the letdown comes. It will be tough, hard. You will face weeks of loneliness.'"

I followed Al for almost five months. He continued to say that God was faithful, even though he did not understand God's ways. It is not necessarily possible to understand what is happening to you and how it will fit into your life. But we do know that there is a source of joy. There is a spirit of thanksgiving. There is a spirit of faith available every day independent of circumstances, independent of people, and of people's choices. On any given day, you have an option. You can submit your life to the Lord,

There is a spirit of faith available every day independent of circumstances, independent of people, and of people's choices.

but you do not have to. You can rejoice, but you do not have to. That leaves with you a daily choice. Which way will you choose?

Giving Thanks in Times of Need

My wife and I attended a conference on the island of Haiti. A missionary pointed out a man who had walked for two days to get there. He lived near the top of a mountain. His people, who all lived in mud huts, were wanting to express their love for God by building Him a church out of cement blocks. The whole community chipped in money to purchase the cement blocks, but they were so poor they could only afford to buy a block or two each month. It would take several more years before they could accumulate enough blocks.

My wife was so moved by this story that she proposed that we supply the money for them to buy the materials to build the church. It only cost a few hundred dollars. We returned home, got caught up in our routines, and forgot about that church.

Many months later we received a letter. The church building was completed and they asked if I would come to see it. So off I went.

A Haitian accompanied me from Port Au Prince to the foot of the mountain. He was educated in the United States but lived in Haiti. Why did he return home? Because, he said, he loved his people. On this trip I learned that love for people is not a matter of education or wealth—or the weather.

It was raining when we started out. We were riding in a four-wheel drive Jeep. I remarked to Claude, the driver, that it was a rough ride. He nodded. We came to a little village where we left the road and followed what looked like a path up toward the mountain. The path got bumpier. The Jeep had seven or eight speeds forward, and Claude shifted from one gear to a lower gear. Soon the path became too difficult to move at all. He shut the motor off and announced that we would walk the rest of the way. It was a relief to leave that extremely bumpy ride. My side ached from hitting the door when the Jeep lurched sideways, and my head hurt from hitting the top.

Fortunately I did have a pair of hiking boots. There was a light rain falling as we began our journey. When we had walked about an hour, we met four men from the community where we were headed. They had come down to escort us up the mountain. They brought a horse for me to ride. I was pleased and relieved. It started raining harder. The next thing I knew my horse had stumbled and I was picking myself up out of a mud puddle.

I had been thinking about a simple Bible verse that had only two words:

Rejoice always.

1 Thess. 5:16

And another that had only four words:

In everything give thanks.

v. 18

I believe it is important for us to keep Bible verses in mind and to recognize that the Bible points to a Spirit that is available to us when we need it. When do you need joy more than when you are starting up a mountain in the rain? Is the joy of the Lord available to you in a puddle after you have fallen off a horse? Worse yet, my companions advised me that I had better walk. I did not know at that point this meant walking for *nine hours* in the rain, sloshing in mud up to my ankles. It was a little, narrow trail, which cattle, horses, and people shared—all in single file up the mountain. On that trail it did not make a bit of difference what my net worth was. What did matter was whether there was communion between God and me. He did give me His joy. I needed an additional infusion of joy when my sense of smell let me know that there was urine and cow dung in that puddle.

I discovered that rejoicing sometimes involves rejoicing when you are hungry, drenched to the skin, and aching. We made it nine hours later. They were so proud of their crude cement block church building.

"Come, let us show you our church," they said.

The walls were crooked and the cement blocks were unrefined but there was a church full of happy, delighted, rejoicing people. The amazing fact is that the resources of God are available to *everybody*.

A committee of people came to me to express their appreciation for the few hundred dollars that my wife and I gave them. You would have thought they had received a grant to build a cathedral.

One man had fourteen children. I remarked that he must grow ten times as many bananas with all those helpers. He shook his head. The amount of land is fixed. Every time there is a new mouth, there is less food. I began to understand what a sacrifice that church was.

I left all my extra clothes there for the people and started down the mountain wearing jeans and a shirt. Allan Morris, who lives in Coral Gables, Florida, met me at the Miami airport on Sunday. There were no stores open so I could not buy any clothes. I went to church with him in a shirt and jeans that I had on for two days.

The pastor spotted me and called me to the platform. I could not believe the contrast. Just two days ago I saw a rugged cement block church, no windows, a cement floor, and benches consisting of a palm tree trunk split down the middle. Here was a decorated room, stained-glass windows, padded pews, and electric lights.

It dawned on me that there is no more love, joy, or peace available to the people in this church than there is to the people on the mountains. We all must reach out an empty hand the same way. The resources of God must be requested.

> **I know how to be abased, and I know how to abound.**
> **Everywhere and in all things I have learned both to be full**
> **and to be hungry, both to abound and to suffer need.**
>
> PHIL. 4:12

Giving Thanks in Times of Prosperity

A major problem in our nation is that we do not know how to have plenty and abound. I am consulting now with a gentleman who set up a trust of $50,000 available to his daughter at age twenty-one. She is spending this money very unwisely. He is frantic about it. How sad. Here is a man who has the ability to generate that kind of money, only to discover that his child is not using it wisely. I have listened to people who are happy and hungry, and people who are miserable and full. Happy are those who know how to do both and yield to the consistent source of love, joy, and peace that is not related to business curves, economics, food, and housing. It involves people and their God. I have had the joy of working with many lost but well-fed and well-housed people and introducing them to the source of power we all need. Whether in an elegant room or in a mountain hut, God is the same and you approach Him the same way.

I was impressed on that trip up the mountain by the uselessness of my education. Physical fitness, good muscle tone, and balance seemed more useful as those people ran up and down that mountain. I marveled at the agility that they had. I relished the sense of gratitude and appreciation those people have for the beautiful, lovely surroundings that are so freely given to everybody. The mountains, the sky, and the grandeur of the world are available to anybody who will lift up his eyes and look.

I remember a man who came to me for help. His wife and he were having difficulties. She was "nervous." She went to see a physician and he said she did not have a medical problem. He called her husband in and told him that his wife needed a change of environment. He, being a very efficient businessman, lifted up a phone, gave a few orders, and a trip to Hawaii was arranged. He went home and said they were leaving for Hawaii.

She said, "I am not going."

He said, "You *are* going."

Can you picture her in their lovely home, packing expensive clothes in expensive suitcases? Can you picture him marching her into the first-class section of the airplane? If she looked out the plane window, there was the same sky that those Haitian people on the mountain saw. Can you picture him marching her out on the sands of Hawaii the next morning? She was not about to enjoy it, and he could not

> *There are some powers that we do not have, and one of them is to give the order to "be happy," "be joyful," "be peaceful."*

make her. There is not enough money in the world to make her happy. There are some powers that we do not have, and one of them is to give the order to "be happy," "be joyful," "be peaceful." There are some things we cannot command, no matter how educated, influential, or wealthy.

The Bible says,

> **And my God shall supply all your need according to His riches in glory by Christ Jesus.**
>
> PHIL. 4:19

God, supply all your needs? The need that He is talking about is not economic—those people up on that mountain have the same needs that we do. The issue is not housing or food; the issue is spiritual. I want to review for you what kind of spirit we need. The Bible calls it the fruit of the Spirit of God. This has nothing to do with other people or with circumstances. This is between you and God.

> **But the fruit of the Spirit is love, joy, peace, longsuffering, kindness, goodness, faithfulness, gentleness, self-control. Against such there is no law.**
>
> GAL. 5:22–23

> **But as many as received Him, to them He gave the right to become children of God, to those who believe in His name.**
>
> JOHN 1:12

It is a matter of making connections. You must make that connection—inviting Christ into your life and then, of course, yielding yourself day by day to Him.

Trusting God When Your Plans Don't Work Out

I was in South America. I traveled two days to get to this jungle outpost. When I got off the airplane, I noted the missionaries who met me knew something that I did not know: the bush pilot who was to take me into the interior was sick, so after traveling all the distance to the edge of this jungle to visit some Indians, I could not go. They were wondering how I would take that. So they very gingerly told me I could not go any further. Did I have access to the joy of the Lord at a time like that? If my heart was full of joy, all they could stir up was my joy. I reassured them that it was all right.

The day came for me to leave. In some of these remote places they have flights twice a week. This missionary came back from the airline office with a worried look on his face. He told me that the plane was not going to land. We stood there under the beautiful Brazilian skies and watched as the plane flew over the little town and was gone. In places where they do not have any landing lights you must get to where you are going before it gets dark. They did not have time to land where we were. That was too bad.

So what does that mean? They said that the next plane would be in a week! The missionaries could take me on a drive through this trackless jungle to a river on the border between Brazil and Guyana. If they could find someone to take me across I might be able to catch a plane to Georgetown and get out that way. So we decided to do that.

I came to Brazil in a big 747 jet and left in a dugout canoe. They said that I could take the vegetable flight to Georgetown. OK, that is great. I did not know what a vegetable route was. There was a long seat like a church pew on one side of this DC–3. The seat had a pipe frame and a piece of canvas. The other side of the plane was filled with cabbage. Did you ever sit alongside a pile of cabbage for three hours? You need a joy that is not your own at a time like that.

In Georgetown I went for a walk that beautiful moonlit night. All of a sudden I felt an arm slip around my throat and I was choking. I felt somebody grab my arm and somebody else hit me around the waist as I was being dragged off the sidewalk. I do not know where I got the strength, but I took those three guys on and dragged them back on the sidewalk. Soon they left me standing there. My billfold and wristwatch were gone. My credit cards were gone. As I saw those three shirts disappearing into the night, my reaction was that they certainly needed to know about the God that I know. That was my attitude, believe it or not.

My next arrival point was Amsterdam, one of the most efficient air terminals there is. I was standing by this fancy conveyor watching the suitcases go by. They all went by. Where was my suitcase? I got mad. I marched into that baggage office and banged my fist on the table. "I want some attention! I want my bag!" I had been all through Brazil, missed my plane, crossed a river, survived the vegetable flight, got myself mugged, and enjoyed it all. All of a sudden it dawned on me that I was furious over *luggage*!

What is my point? Joy belongs to God. Sometimes you think you are walking in the Spirit and you are not.

> **For if anyone thinks himself to be something, when he is nothing, he deceives himself.**
>
> GAL. 6:3

I had forgotten to practice my nine words. We get these unexpected glimpses of ourselves once in a while. How do you get back to where you need to be in your relationship to God? You repent. I breathed a prayer of repentance, "I am sorry God, will You forgive me? Restore to me the joy of Your salvation."

When I got back home the mission executive was relieved that I made a pleasant adventure out of it. I believe that is one of the most important roles that pastors can play—for people to recognize that somebody who faces many problems can be decent all the time.

There are few things that are free. One of them is the salvation of the Lord and the other one is the power of God. The only way we can have them is to submit ourselves. Could it be that you're reading this and you need to take time right now to invite Christ to come into your life? If you try and use your influence and your authority to order Him to come into your life, it will not work. Why not just *ask* Him? Do it before something comes along and swipes the idea out of your mind. Perhaps you're a Christian but your heart has grown cold. Would you take time right now to talk to the Lord about your heart and life? Please do so before continuing.

HENRY T. BLACKABY

What a wonderfully helpful word has been given to us by Henry Brandt, a faithful and loving layman who trusts his Lord completely. He lives just like he has shared. I have been with him, know a little of his pilgrimage, and appreciate his transparent honesty, a welcome reminder of our faithful God.

> *It seemed foolish to choose my weakness over His strength; my ignorance over His wisdom; my sin over His righteousness; my stress over His peace; and my burdens over His yoke.*

Over the almost thirty years serving as a pastor, the twenty-five years as a father of five children, and a leader among God's choicest people for more than fourteen years, I have had many occasions to confront the reality of my personal relationship with God. I knew in my head all the Bible verses that I should live by. But I needed to know the God of those verses being real and personal in me—in real situations. I had to experience Him being for me what He promised. The choice was mine, not God's. He had already given the promises. I now had to receive them. I had a real choice. I could choose to believe Him, and live by His promises and the life He would bring to my life. I remembered what God had said in Deuteronomy 30:19–20. He had set before me in His Word, life and blessing, death and cursing—and He had urged me to "choose life that you and your descendants would live." This was clear. A child could understand it! Why did it seem so difficult in the real everyday life? It seemed foolish to choose my weakness over His strength; my ignorance over His wisdom; my sin over His righteousness; my stress over His peace; and my burdens over His yoke.

KEEPING THE CHOICE

I made the choice as a young boy. Now I am a grown man with five children, eight grandchildren, and a life filled with responsibilities and opportunities. God led me to realize that He was God and I wasn't! I seek to always remember that, especially when I am in His Presence and in difficult circumstances. I choose to seek always to turn to Him first. It is continuously a deliberate choice I make, and I have kept that choice to this day. I settled it in my heart.

I knew in my head all the Bible verses that I should live by. But I needed to know the God of those verses being real and personal in me— in real situations.

God's Best for Me

I settled in my heart that, since God's very nature is perfect love, He could never relate to me at any time except in perfect love. This meant God would always bring me His best. This was especially true when I faced a major decision as a young man. All my life I admired my uncle, who was a Spitfire pilot in the Canadian Air Force during World War II. I always wanted to fly. However, I had an accident and have only about 10 percent vision in one eye. I would not fly. While in university I applied to be a chaplain in the Air Force. This seemed certain—but I realized I would have to spend time for several years after university in military service. My application was turned down after I felt so certain it would be accepted. It was then I learned of Golden Gate Baptist Theological Seminary in California where I felt compelled of God to go immediately following university to get my theological training. I did, and God led me to a lifetime of involvement with Southern Baptists, led me to a roommate who included me in his wedding, where I met the bride's sister, Marilynn, whom I married. And now the rest is history! My life has been shaped by that solitary moment—God had given me His best when He prevented me from my will and revealed to me His will. I believed Him and obeyed Him.

God's Wisdom for Me

I settled in my heart that God has by nature all wisdom and knowledge, and to have Him is to have His wisdom for my life. This meant when God is involved with me, it is always right. I settled this. I chose to believe and live by this. I do not argue with God, as if my wisdom is better than His or my ways better than His.

Marilynn and I could never have raised four teenage boys at one time and guide them through such difficult times without the wisdom of God. It also took this same wisdom to guide our one daughter through her teenage years, with all that she would face. Many times I did not know what to say or do with my children. I turned instinctively to God. He listened and heard and guided us. As a pastor, in pioneer missions, in a small church, I prayed, "Oh, Lord! We are so poor. I love my children and want Your best for them. Will You either provide for us all I want to give to my children, or help them not to know they are poor?" God chose the latter—for them not to know we were poor. God met our every need. We never went without essentials. My children rarely ever complained. They were happy growing up in a poor pastor's home.

When one of my sons, years later, returned at Christmas from his first semester of his third year in college in the U.S., he said, "Dad, this semester I realized for the first time we were poor when I was young!" I cried and told him what I had prayed, asking God to do His best for us—and He had! And He always has been right in His expressed love toward me.

God's Sufficiency for Me

I settled in my heart that God is sovereign and all-powerful and nothing is impossible with Him (Luke 1:37). I chose to trust Him in all things and at all times. Throughout my life, God has in ever-enlarging ways affirmed Himself to me in such Scriptures as 2 Corinthians 1:20; 2; 9:8; Romans 8; Philippians; and Ephesians 3.

This has been a constant daily choice. This choice by nature involves

- denying self,
- taking up my cross,
- following Him.

FOLLOWING GOD'S WILL

Each time I have faced a change in where I would serve God, it seemed we took a drastic salary cut and had another child. On both counts, I did not want to move again. But in each of the times we moved to another church or situation, God brought us into new and fresh experiences of Himself and His provision, greater than we had ever known.

In seeking to encourage my wife, Marilynn, to move with peace and joy from southern California and all the warmth and security we enjoyed to Saskatoon, Saskatchewan, Canada, I assured her most every home there had a fireplace. I described the joys of a fireplace on cold winter days. We moved into a parsonage with no fireplace! For twelve long years we had *no fireplace!* Then we moved to Vancouver, and to my amazement the house that was rented for us had three fireplaces! Marilynn smiled and put her head down and said, "Henry, this time I was not leaving it to you. I asked God to give me three fireplaces, and He did!"

Many times I felt I knew what was best for me, yet it never came about. Instead, something very different came. I then had to make a conscious choice—to believe in God's love, His wisdom, and His presence to guide and direct my life. I chose to follow Him no matter what my senses were indicating or my reasoning was doing. In the little things and the big things, God is faithful, God is able.

Shortly after I moved to Atlanta, Georgia, as Director of the Office of Prayer and Spiritual Awakening, I had to select an associate to work with me. I felt inadequate. I began to put my best thinking to the task of this selection. I thought of a person who was a good preacher, a strong personality, an experienced leader, etc. Then God brought across my life Ron and Patricia Owens—who were singers. All their life they had spent in music and singing in the Lord's work. God assured me, "Here is My choice for your associate!"

But Lord—

"Here is My choice. I have been shaping their lives to this very day, for just such a time and place."

I obeyed—and God was right! Never have I worked with two persons God had so perfectly matched to all I was doing—and more important, all we were going to do. They together wrote and sang music to match *Experiencing God* and *Fresh Encounter* (which I wrote with Claude King). And God called and equipped Ron to preach, teach, and lead conferences and write—and do all we have needed before we even knew what we would be doing! God exceeds far more abundantly than we could even have known to request.

REJOICING IN GOD'S WILL

These words of instruction are foundational to my personal walk with God, for my family, and for my ministry:

Rejoice always, pray without ceasing, in everything give thanks; for this is the will of God in Christ Jesus for you.

1 THESS. 5:16–18

While in seminary, I was asked to serve as a Music/Education Director in our church. I loved it! I could have done this the rest of my life. Then our pastor became ill and I was asked to become their pastor. "Not my will, but Thine, oh Lord" was my prayer response. Nervous and scared (I had preached only three times in my life), I became pastor. I loved it and could do this for the rest of my life.

Then God "called" Marilynn and me to release our lives to foreign missions. We did so gladly, trusting God. But as we finished our application process our oldest son became ill and we were asked to wait two years because of his health. "Not our will, but Thine be done, oh Lord," was my response. We watched for God's directive with joy, not with disappointment. Our call was to Him, not to an assignment.

God led us to Canada and a small church of ten discouraged people. In the next eighteen years we experienced more of God and His love, grace, and power than all our life put together. Out of those years came our witness to Him through the book I wrote called *Experiencing God: Knowing and Doing the Will of God*. Indescribable is the only word that can capture the fullness of God experienced since then.

God guided us in the same way to leave being a pastor of a church which Marilynn and I have loved deeply, and become a Director of Missions (guiding a regional group of churches), and then to the Home Mission Board (now the North American Mission Board) in Atlanta, where I have served for the last eight years as Director of the Office of Prayer and Spiritual Awakening, and finally to be added to the Foreign Mission Board and the Baptist Sunday School Board as a consultant for Revival and Spiritual Awakening. I could never have planned this. Only God could!

God's ways are not our ways, and I am grateful. His ways are always best and always right and always with His fullness!

This is time to renew our relationship with God and choose to believe Him. It is crucial, in my life, and in yours, to once again hear the words of the Lord:

Let him deny himself, and take up his cross daily, and follow Me.

LUKE 9:23

PROCESS THE MESSAGE

1. Is there an area of your life in which you need to learn to rejoice always? If so, what area?

2. Is there an area of your life in which you need to learn to pray without ceasing and give thanks always? If so, what area?

3. Do you need to return to God in some other area of your life?

4. What will you do next about what God has shown you while reading this chapter?

PART FOUR

God's Standard for Your Ministry

ELEVEN

Taking Spiritual Inventory

> But we have this treasure in earthen vessels, that the
> excellence of the power may be of God and not of us.
> 2 CORINTHIANS 4:7
>
> It could well be that some of us are the authors and the
> creators of our own inner turmoil, simply because we
> reason apart from the Scriptures.
> HENRY BRANDT
>
> Too often we listen to the reasoning of the world that tells
> us, "Tension in the ministry is normal," "Don't worry, it
> will all work out somehow!" But sadly, this is often the
> beginning of a heart turning from God.
> HENRY T. BLACKABY

HENRY BRANDT

Years ago I addressed a group of missionaries in Brazil. I am sure that people in Brazil are like people everywhere else. They are looking for real peace, real joy, something that they can put their hearts into—not something that they are repelled by, but must do anyway. There are some standards that the Lord set for us as far as our performance is concerned.

Many people say that the missionary should not think of himself as being on a level above the people he came to minister to. I should think that if you are a missionary, you should have achieved some higher ground. There is a sense in which you can say to people, "Follow my example, come up here."

> **Follow my example, as I follow the example of Christ.**
>
> 1 COR. 11:1, NIV

> **Remember those who rule over you, who have spoken the word of God to you, whose faith follow, considering the outcome of their conduct.**
>
> HEB. 13:7

Maybe *up* is not the right term, but there is such a thing as helping a person who is filled with apprehension to find some release from it. In that sense it is "Come up." It is not that you are superior to anyone, but that you have found something that you want to share with them. Sympathetic understanding, in the sense that you are in the same predicament they are, is not much help. But sympathetic understanding in the sense that you can understand their dilemma because you, too, have been in your share of predicaments and have found your way out—that they need to hear!

CONSTANT IMPROVEMENT

When I was working for General Motors Corporation, I was subjected to an evaluation every six months. Obviously, there were some things that I did well, but there were always things that I could have done better. After that evaluation, I always ended up with a plan to improve my performance. I despised those evaluations, but they were some of the best experiences that ever happened to me.

All of us ought to be consciously and knowingly doing something to improve. We should be able to look back and see that we have improved. That is not pride. It could be, but it does not have to be. It can be a fact. You might have actually added to your knowledge; you might be easier to live with. On the other hand, you might have slipped. That is good to know too—provided you will do something about it. If you caught a glimpse of yourself and all you have done is turn away, you will be disturbed. That is all. You will not have much to offer anybody else, except the pattern of getting a glimpse of yourself and ignoring it.

What we need to learn is the pattern of taking an honest look at ourselves, repenting, and actually seeing some change. That is, you must confess your sins. These three words must be taken seriously:

Sin is lawlessness.

1 JOHN 3:4

I am very happy if I can diagnose sin in somebody's life, because sin is one of the simplest problems there is to deal with. We know from our own experience that the blood of Jesus Christ will cleanse our hearts from sin. Is that just a figure of speech, or is that an experience that you had, and have? As you acknowledge sin in your life, the blood of Jesus Christ will wash it away. We are dealing in the realm of the miraculous, not just the academic or the intellectual.

You can describe what you are like and argue that it is perfectly valid for you to be that way, even though the Bible says you should not. You say, "I should get some credit for talking about it." Is it not curious that people would want to cling to their sins rather than give them up? People tell me that they are scientific, objective, and open because they talk freely about their sins. Just talking about sin and leaving it there is not enough. That is step number one, and it is necessary, but step number two is equally necessary. That is saying, "I am sorry. I am repentant. This is wrong. I admit it. I must be free of this. I am in search of help. Yes, I am sinful, and I am not blaming anybody either."

> *What we need to learn is the pattern of taking an honest look at ourselves, repenting, and actually seeing some change.*

FINDING JOY WHERE YOU ARE

In Financially Trying Times

I have people coming to me these days as anxious people, worried about money and the future. They start out telling me, "I was reared in the Depression." This Depression experience is the cause of their present condition, they say.

I was in high school during the Depression. We had a neighbor who was a highly skilled tool-and-die maker. He made a lot of money, and suddenly he was out of work. He would come over to our house and sit on the veranda and visit, for a change. I remember him saying that it looked as though the Lord was going to take all his resources away from him—his home and everything. He was wondering what the Lord was up to. He was just curious. Then he would get to talking about the sunset and say, "My, it has been a long time since I have had time to enjoy a sunset." I learned to appreciate sunsets. The Depression did not stop the sun from setting. The loss of a job and property did not hinder my neighbor's faith in God.

I remember the day that neighbor said, "I am going on welfare. I have a job on the WPA digging ditches." He came home the next day with a new shovel, acting like a kid with a new toy. He explained to us why you need to buy this kind of a shovel in order to dig a good ditch. That man got me so interested in ditches that I actually went to watch him work. I saw some very disgruntled, grumpy, angry men, leaning on their shovels and cursing God, the world, and their circumstances. In that very same spot there were a few people who were happily digging a ditch as unto the Lord.

That man, and my parents, taught me that you do not need to be afraid of a depression. It does not matter if you lose your home, does it? That loss does not hinder your walk in the Spirit.

In Challenging Circumstances

Another learning experience came as I was flying in a seaplane with a mission executive off the coast of British Columbia. As we were coming down to a little island where his mission had a work among the Indians, he told me a story that had happened just a few months before. He had gone to the island to visit two missionary couples. The first said, "Oh, are we glad to see you. My, what a terrible place this is. These Indian children curse and swear, and they are dirty and filthy. They have lice, and now our children have lice. These people are unfriendly. We are so lonely here. It is a terrible place."

Then he went down the street to visit the other missionary couple. A young man opened the door. He was dirty, his face was all smudgy, and he said, "Come on in. I am glad to see you. Our stove just blew up." He led the way into the house and said, "Look at this place. This was a nice, neat place just a few minutes ago. Amazing what can happen when an oil stove blows up." Then he said, "Do you want to go fishing? I have found some good fishing holes." He told how he made friends with some Indians, and they showed him all their favorite fishing holes. He said, "You know, these people are hard to reach. What a challenge! This is great!" Remember, this is the same island!

People go to other lands in the name of the Lord, and some curse the country: "Oh, the tensions, pressures, problems, and the difficulties in this country." There are other people who talk about the wonderful challenge in the same country: "It is great just to be here!"

In Whatever You Do

And whatever you do in word or deed, do all in the name of the Lord Jesus, giving thanks to God the Father through Him.

COL. 3:17

Is that possible? Is this just a tantalizing idea that God allowed to be put into His Book to make life miserable for us, and to make us more uncomfortable? We can attain a spirit of thanksgiving and a sense of ministry as unto the Lord. This *is* a possibility for anybody who knows Christ.

There are people who say, "Do you expect me to enjoy this work? If my boss thought I enjoyed this job, I would be stuck with it forever. The only way to get out of this job is to let people know how unhappy I am." What a tragedy. Missionaries and pastors are ministering to people who will not find themselves in ideal situations. If they are to find a thankful spirit, they need to find it where they are.

Is there such a thing as finding joy where you are? Is there such a thing as doing what you have committed yourself to do, or you have been assigned to do, with thanksgiving in your heart? I did not say with resentment in your heart. I did not say repulsed by the job. What job? Any job.

Everyone has to do some things he would rather not do. But since he must do it, he can do it as unto the Lord with thanksgiving. Many times you have the privilege of making a choice. You can legitimately say, "No, thank you, I do not care to do it." But I am talking about a job you *must* do. It is yours.

And whatever you do, do it heartily, as to the Lord and not to men.

COL. 3:23

If you do not put your heart into it, it is because you elect not to— not because there are no resources available for you. It could well be that some of us are the authors and the creators of our own inner turmoil, simply because we reason apart from the Scriptures.

But we have this treasure in earthen vessels, that the excellence of the power may be of God and not of us.

2 COR. 4:7

You see, we are talking about something that comes from God, not an arrangement of people, not fortunate situations. Paul described how to respond to life by walking in the Spirit:

We are hard pressed on every side, yet not crushed; we are perplexed, but not in despair; persecuted, but not forsaken; struck down, but not destroyed.

2 COR. 4:8–9

DIFFICULT TIMES

You can describe what you are like and argue that it is perfectly valid for you to be that way, even though the Bible says you should not.

There is no promise of a smooth life. Mine has not been. Jesus Himself said that in this world we would have trouble, and He went right on to say, "Be of good cheer," as much as to say, "Enjoy it. I have overcome the world. You can, too." Imagine having trouble on every side, and not being distressed. If you can teach people that there is such a possibility, you have given them a pearl of great value.

We all face our share of perplexities. I have talked to puzzled parents who scratched their heads saying, "What will I do with that boy? What will I do with that girl? What will I do with my partner?" Sometimes when a man describes his marriage partner to me, I am glad it is his marriage partner and not mine. I have had to say to some couples, "I have news for you. What you need is a lifetime of grace."

You can be perplexed, but not in despair. You can be persecuted. I must be writing to someone who is persecuted. You have somebody on your back. Nobody ever had it like you. You are all alone. Have you ever felt that way?

Cast Down but Not Destroyed

I was in the Congo in 1964, just a few months before the uprising. I had friends who were persecuted. Do you know what they did to my interpreter? They chopped her up and threw her in the river to crocodiles. Do you know what they did to one man? They tied his hands behind his back, tied his ankles together, bent him in a backward arc and tied his ankles to his wrists. Then somebody took a beer bottle and laced his arms, and then worked over his backbone until he died. He could not do a thing about it. Then they threw him to the crocodiles too.

Some of my friends were imprisoned. I have since been in meetings where those very same men were in prayer. I participated in helping those men make plans to go back to minister to the people who did it. That lady who knows they smashed her husband's eyes out and knocked off his nose, and cut him to ribbons and threw him in the river—do you suppose there is enough love available from God for her so that she could love the people who did it? She will tell you there is.

I was standing by in New York, ready to receive these people that we were sure would be on the edge of insanity. Praise God, those people did not need me! They found out that you can open your heart to the grace and comfort of God when you are in prison, with your nose pressed in the dust, and bullets flying over your head. That is the gospel for you.

Some of us have had that experience, where people have said, "Get out. We do not want anything to do with you." You have gone to places where they have isolated you. Cast down, but not destroyed.

Always carrying about in the body the dying of the Lord Jesus, that the life of Jesus also may be manifested in our body.

2 Cor. 4:10

Responding to Despair

Did you ever consider how a person acts who is distressed? These are the people who wring their hands, pace the floor, get up and sit down, scratch their heads—they are distressed! Their blood pressure is up, the heart beat is up, respiration is up. These are the people who walk into my office holding their chests, gasping, "The doctor said there is nothing wrong, but, oh, my chest hurts!"

Physicians talk about seeking a state called homeostasis. Balance. There is a norm for your heartbeat, and your blood pressure, and your digestive system. There is a norm as far as muscular relaxation is concerned.

The man who walks in the Spirit is relaxed and comfortable. The psalmist says,

> **I will both lie down in peace, and sleep;**
> **For You alone, O LORD, make me dwell in safety.**
>
> Ps. 4:8

When your faith is in the Lord, what do you care how it turns out? I have seen people who have been in all kinds of trouble find their way out. I have come to realize that the proper attitude toward trouble is, "I am fascinated to see how God will help me solve my problems." But how do you solve them? Happily, or all tense and tied up into knots?

People in despair are the ones who drag themselves into my office and say, "I could hardly get out of bed this morning. I am tired." Their blood pressure is down, their heartbeat is down. Life is pretty rough. These are the people who find something wrong everywhere. "If I could just get out of this country and get back to the United States," says the unhappy missionary. I will guarantee he will find something wrong with the USA before he gets out of customs. That is not the person who walks in the Spirit.

Why do we insist on being miserable? Why do we argue that it is normal and natural to be filled with apprehensions and fears and conflicts within? Sometimes our difficulties and fears become like precious antiques. We love to talk about them, but we would not give them up for anything. There is a question in Romans that we must ask ourselves, unless we want to ignore it:

Who shall separate us from the love of Christ? Shall tribulation, or distress, or persecution, or famine, or nakedness, or peril, or sword?

ROM. 8:35

I was in Haiti one time, and I saw some healthy-looking people with rosy cheeks. It looked as though they were well fed. It was pointed out to me that these people were in the last stages of starvation. They were naked and hungry. After being there a few weeks, it was tremendous to get back to the States. Somebody met me in Miami and whisked me off in a nice Oldsmobile convertible. We went to a big cafeteria, and lining the wall was every kind of salad, meat, vegetable, and dessert. We had to stand in line a few minutes, and to my amazement, I heard people complain because we had to stand in line.

I realized as I came home from that trip that there in Haiti, where people were in rags and starving, there were happy people and unhappy people. And in my own country, where everybody has all they can eat, there are happy people and there are unhappy people. It is not nakedness or famine or persecution that separates you from the love of God.

Yet in all these things we are more than conquerors through Him who loved us.

ROM. 8:37

God's Resource

This is our message. We have a resource available to us, and it is from God. It has to do with our communion with God. Now, as far as the future is concerned, what will help us communicate this message? You need to sense this power in your own life.

When people get acquainted with the inner workings of your mission, can they say, "Behold, how they love one another"? I think it is basic that you must resolve your own issues between yourselves. People with songs of thanksgiving in their hearts are able to admonish their brethren, *and* are able to submit one to another. There is such a thing as being of one mind and one spirit. You do not need to have stalemates in your organization. I think of a leader as one who loves people just as they are and teaches them what the Word of God has to say about living together.

There is a very challenging passage of Scripture in Philippians. The first time I read this I thought to myself that if you tried to compose a more egotistical statement than this, you could not do it:

> **The things which you learned and received and heard and saw in me, these do, and the God of peace will be with you.**
>
> PHIL. 4:9

How is that for egotism? "Watch me. If you turn out like me, you will be OK." But we should finish the verse. "And the God of peace will be with you [as He is with me]". If you have not tapped that resource, you will soon discover that this verse is not an egotistical statement. It is a description of how you will behave if empowered by God.

HENRY T. BLACKABY

In the years that I have served as a pastor, there was a word of encouragement from Jesus that always helped me—and still does:

> **Come to Me, all you who labor and are heavy laden, and I will give you rest. Take My yoke upon you and learn from Me, for I am gentle and lowly in heart, and you will find rest for your souls. For My yoke is easy and My burden is light.**
>
> MATT. 11:28–30

This is an invitation from God. It is addressed to specific people. It is for those who realize and recognize they have a real, personal need in their lives that God can correct. If my life, my family, my marriage, and my ministry are becoming burdensome and too heavy for me to carry, I need to "come" to my Lord Jesus, and

- take His yoke upon me,
- learn from Him.

I have regularly and systematically done this. God has always done for me what He promised! After many years and to this day I have found "rest to my soul." While I have been regularly doing this, I have become aware of others who are in "burnout." They have left the ministry full of anxiety and fear, experiencing loss, failure, and brokenness. They complain that "this is a most difficult time for pastors!"

How is it possible to

Be anxious for nothing, but in everything by prayer and supplication, with thanksgiving, let your requests be made known to God; and the peace of God, which surpasses all understanding, will guard your hearts and minds through Christ Jesus.

PHIL. 4:6–7

A GODLY HABIT

It is crucial that a servant of God regularly take spiritual inventory of his walk with and relationship to God. At the very first sign of difficulty, or change of heart, make an immediate correction back to God's original plan. When the joy is diminishing or strained, go immediately to these passages: John 15:9–12; 16:22–24; 1 Thessalonians 5:16; Romans 15:13; Galatians 5:22–23; 1 Peter 1:8.

It is crucial that a servant of God regularly take spiritual inventory of his walk with and relationship to God.

Too often we listen to the reasoning of the world that tells us, "Tension in the ministry is normal," "Don't worry, it will all work out somehow!" But sadly, this is often the beginning of a heart turning from God. This leads to ever-increasing frustration, rationalizing, and ultimate brokenness. To avoid this, take a spiritual inventory regularly. It can be a habit in your life as you

- *read* God's Word and experience "the washing of water by the word" (Eph. 5:26);
- *pray* (see what happened to Isaiah in Isa. 6:1–8);
- *worship* (see John in Rev. 1:10–20);
- *encounter God* as Moses did (Exod. 3:1–6), or Peter, James, and John (Luke 5:1–11), or Saul of Tarsus (Acts 9:1–9).

The one who regularly chooses to meditate on God's Word, day and night, is the one whose

delight is in the law of the LORD
And in His law he meditates day and night.
He shall be like a tree
Planted by the rivers of water,
That brings forth its fruit in its season,
Whose leaf also shall not wither;
And whatever he does shall prosper.

Ps. 1:2–3

GOD'S PLUMB LINES

Regularly placing your life alongside God's plumb lines (Amos 7:7–8) will help you to know if matters of relationship with God, especially as a shepherd, are shifting or changing.

Do this test regularly to see what I mean. The following guidelines for a "true shepherd" are taken from the Bible. Read these Scriptures, meditate on God's plumb lines, then respond to the spiritual inventory that follows. These plumb lines will allow you to stand before God and let Him reveal if you are "measuring up" or if your heart is departing:

> **"Let the LORD, the God of the spirits of all flesh, set a man over the congregation, who may go out before them and go in before them, who may lead them out and bring them in, that the congregation of the LORD may not be like sheep which have no shepherd."**

NUM. 27:16–17

> **He also chose David His servant,**
> **And took him from the sheepfolds;**
> **From following the ewes that had young He brought him,**
> **To shepherd Jacob His people,**
> **And Israel His inheritance.**
> **So he shepherded them according to the integrity of his heart,**
> **And guided them by the skillfulness of his hands.**

Ps. 78:70–72

> **For the shepherds have become dull-hearted, And have not**
> **sought the LORD; Therefore they shall not prosper,**
> **And all their flocks shall be scattered.**

JER. 10:21

	MY LIFE		
God's True Shepherd	**Always**	**Sometimes**	**Rarely**
1. Has integrity before God for each of them (they are His)			
2. Leads in love—gently, patiently, kindly			
3. Uses all resources for the benefit of the sheep			
4. Goes in and out before the sheep (guides them safely)			
5. Protects and watches over them			
6. Pays attention to each member's lifestyle			
7. Stays alert to the call from God			

"Woe to the shepherds who destroy and scatter the sheep of My pasture!" says the LORD. Therefore thus says the LORD God of Israel against the shepherds who feed My people: "You have scattered My flock, driven them away, and not attended to them. Behold, I will attend to you for the evil of your doings," says the LORD. "But I will gather the remnant of My flock out of all countries where I have driven them, and bring them back to their folds; and they shall be fruitful and increase. I will set up shepherds over them who will feed them; and they shall fear no more, nor be dismayed, nor shall they be lacking," says the LORD.

JER. 23:1–4

	MY LIFE		
God's True Shepherd	**Always**	**Sometimes**	**Rarely**
1. Faithfully feeds the flock with the Word of God			
2. Comforts			
3. Creates an atmosphere free from fear			
4. Keeps the sheep from scattering			
5. Stays vigilant			

Thus says the LORD of hosts: "Do not listen to the words of
the prophets who prophesy to you.
They make you worthless;
They speak a vision of their own heart,
Not from the mouth of the LORD. They continually say to
those who despise Me,
'The LORD has said, "You shall have peace"';
And to everyone who walks according to the dictates of his
own heart, they say,
'No evil shall come upon you.'"
For who has stood in the counsel of the LORD,
And has perceived and heard His word?
Who has marked His word and heard it?
"But if they had stood in My counsel,
And had caused My people to hear My words,
Then they would have turned them from their evil way
And from the evil of their doings.
The prophet who has a dream, let him tell a dream;
And he who has My word, let him speak My word faithfully.
What is the chaff to the wheat?" says the LORD.
"Is not My word like a fire?" says the LORD,
"And like a hammer that breaks the rock in pieces?
Therefore behold, I am against the prophets," says the LORD,
"who steal My words every one from his neighbor. Behold, I
am against the prophets," says the LORD, "who use their
tongues and say, 'He says.'"

JER. 23:16–18, 22, 28–31

	MY LIFE		
God's True Shepherd	Always	Sometimes	Rarely
1. Protects from error			
2. Restores the wayward			
3. Turns them from their evil ways			
4. Leads with righteousness			
5. Warns and alerts them to danger— e.g., false teachers			
6. Preaches a vision of the heart			
7. Watches over his own heart			

And Jesus, when He came out, saw a great multitude and was moved with compassion for them, because they were like sheep not having a shepherd. So He began to teach them many things.

MARK 6:34

"What man of you, having a hundred sheep, if he loses one of them, does not leave the ninety-nine in the wilderness, and go after the one which is lost until he finds it? And when he has found it, he lays it on his shoulders, rejoicing. And when he comes home, he calls together his friends and neighbors, saying to them, 'Rejoice with me, for I have found my sheep which was lost!' I say to you that likewise there will be more joy in heaven over one sinner who repents than over ninety-nine just persons who need no repentance."

LUKE 15:4–7

	MY LIFE		
God's True Shepherd	Always	Sometimes	Rarely
1. Teaches them from the Word			
2. Protects and watches over the flock			
3. Finds/seeks the lost and the straying			
4. Carries some of the sheep			

"But he who enters by the door is the shepherd of the sheep. To him the doorkeeper opens, and the sheep hear his voice; and he calls his own sheep by name and leads them out. And when he brings out his own sheep, he goes before them; and the sheep follow him, for they know his voice. Yet they will by no means follow a stranger, but will flee from him, for they do not know the voice of strangers. . . . I am the good shepherd. The good shepherd gives His life for the sheep. But a hireling, he who is not the shepherd, one who does not own the sheep, sees the wolf coming and leaves the sheep and flees; and the wolf catches the sheep and scatters them. The hireling flees because he is a hireling and does not care about the sheep. I am the good shepherd; and I know My

sheep, and am known by My own. As the Father knows Me,
even so I know the Father; and I lay down My life for the
sheep."

JOHN 10:2–5, 11–15

	MY LIFE		
God's True Shepherd	Always	Sometimes	Rarely
1. Takes time to know and pattern his life after the Great Shepherd			
2. Selfless—even laying down his life for them if needed			
3. Does not drive them, but leads them			
4. Places the interests of sheep above his own			

This is a faithful saying: If a man desires the position of a
bishop, he desires a good work. A bishop then must be
blameless, the husband of one wife, temperate, sober-
minded, of good behavior, hospitable, able to teach; not
given to wine, not violent, not greedy for money, but gentle,
not quarrelsome, not covetous; one who rules his own house
well, having his children in submission with all reverence (for
if a man does not know how to rule his own house, how will
he take care of the church of God?); not a novice, lest being
puffed up with pride he fall into the same condemnation as
the devil. Moreover he must have a good testimony among
those who are outside, lest he fall into reproach and the
snare of the devil.

1 TIM. 3:1–7

Do not wait until everything is "falling apart." The parable of the ten
virgins (Matt. 25:1–13) gives a vivid picture of five being "too late."
They lost everything they had been called to do.

Another way to take inventory and know if your life, ministry, family,
and marriage is all God has purposed and called you to be, is to

- read key Scriptures or promises;
- meditate on the full implications of the Truth for your life;

	MY LIFE		
God's True Shepherd	**Always**	**Sometimes**	**Rarely**
1. Blameless toward them			
2. Of good behavior, hospitable; not given to wine			
3. Able to teach			
4. Not greedy for money			
5. Gentle			
6. Not quarrelsome			
7. Not covetous			
8. One who rules his own house well			

- measure with transparent honesty—in God's sight—where your life is in relation to all God has promised would be real and personal in you.

Read the following Scriptures carefully and honestly: Deuteronomy 6:1–9; 9:12–21; 30:19–20; Psalms 15; 25:8–15; 50:15; Isaiah 41:9–10; Matthew 6:33–34; 7:7–8; 16:15–19; John 14:12–18; 15:1–17; 16:7–15; 17:1–26; Acts 1:8; 2 Corinthians 1:20; 9:8; Ephesians 1:3–6, 17–23; 3:14–21; Philippians 1:6; 2:5–11; 3:10; 4:6–9, 13, 19; Colossians 1:12–13; 2:9–10.

Often we are the source of our own frustrations and brokenness. It is a matter of our heart. No one, or no circumstances, can change my heart. My heart is under my control. I must follow this Scripture:

Keep your heart with all diligence,
For out of it spring the issues of life.

PROV. 4:23

No one can make me angry. This is a choice I make. And I do not need to remain angry. I can immediately recognize it as sin, repent of it, receive God's wonderful cleansing and forgiveness, and, knowing the truth, be free!

Then Jesus said to those Jews who believed Him, "If you abide in My word, you are My disciples indeed. And you shall know the truth, and the truth shall make you free."

JOHN 8:31–32

Summing up many things, it is good to remember constantly, and live in the light of, Peter's assurance:

> **To the elect according to the foreknowledge of God the Father, in sanctification of the Spirit, for obedience and sprinkling of the blood of Jesus Christ: Grace to you and peace be multiplied. Blessed be the God and Father of our Lord Jesus Christ, who according to His abundant mercy has begotten us again to a living hope through the resurrection of Jesus Christ from the dead, to an inheritance incorruptible and undefiled and that does not fade away, reserved in heaven for you, who are kept by the power of God through faith for salvation ready to be revealed in the last time. In this you greatly rejoice, though now for a little while, if need be, you have been grieved by various trials, that the genuineness of your faith, being much more precious than gold that perishes, though it is tested by fire, may be found to praise, honor, and glory at the revelation of Jesus Christ, whom having not seen you love. Though now you do not see Him, yet believing, you rejoice with joy inexpressible and full of glory, receiving the end of your faith—the salvation of your souls. Of this salvation the prophets have inquired and searched carefully, who prophesied of the grace that would come to you, searching what, or what manner of time, the Spirit of Christ who was in them was indicating when He testified beforehand the sufferings of Christ and the glories that would follow.**
>
> 1 PET. 1:1–11

These words are wonderful—if—knowing God's assurances for our life and ministry, we adjust anything and everything that does not "measure up" to this, asking the Spirit of God to work in us until every word is true in experience and life.

P R O C E S S   T H E   M E S S A G E

1. Did God speak to you of your strengths and weaknesses as a shepherd while you read His Word in this chapter? If so, how do you need to respond?

2. Are there people or difficult church situations that you blame for your present condition?

3. Would you ask God to forgive you of any sin that you have as a result of blaming others?

4. Why is it hard to measure your life against Scripture and at the same time not give justifying reasons for your condition?

TWELVE

The Distraction of the World's Methods

> See to it that no one carries you off as spoil or makes you yourselves captive by his so-called philosophy and intellectualism and vain deceit (idle fancies and plain nonsense), following human tradition (men's ideas of the material rather than the spiritual world), just crude notions following the rudimentary and elemental teaching of the universe and disregarding [the teachings of] Christ (the Messiah). For in Him the whole fullness of Deity (the Godhead) continues to dwell in bodily form [giving complete expression of the divine nature].
>
> COLOSSIANS 2:8, AMP

> More and more frequently pastors say to me, "Doc, I am thinking of leaving the ministry. How can I get in on what you are doing? You see, I have only studied theology and the Bible. How can I help people like you do?" What a pity to hear a pastor refer to himself that way: "I only studied theology and the Bible."
>
> HENRY BRANDT

> Please, never exchange the world's ways (which are not real ways) for God's ways. It would be fatal to you and to those who come to you for help.
>
> HENRY T. BLACKABY

HENRY BRANDT

After World War II, thousands of restless, anxious, unhappy soldiers returned to our shores. They returned to their churches and were faced with standards, rules, and guidelines for Christian living. They heard sermons about sin, the need for repentance, and the forgiveness of sin.

Many of these soldiers turned to counseling centers for help. They reported that the church made them feel guilty and unclean. Non-Christian counselors pressured pastors to change their message and their standards. Preaching about sin and Christian living was thought to be creating a nation of neurotics. Non-Christians said that people need to be loved, understood, and accepted as they are. Who understood how to do this? Why, the psychiatrists, psychologists, social workers, and educators. Pastors were taught that they should learn to help people by following the leading of the social sciences. The church's teachings just led to frustration and neurosis. The church's influence did not keep us out of World War II, did it? Such was the pressure from the church's critics. Some of you remember those days; others need to know what happened in those days.

RISE OF THE SOCIAL SCIENCES

Pastors by the droves turned to all kinds of books on psychology, sociology, social work, counseling, psychiatry, and anthropology. This also happened in the seminaries. Pastors and students filled their heads with the views of people who either did not know what was in the Bible or who rejected it.

In the early 1960s there were some warning signs in our society. Crime rates were growing, juvenile delinquencies were on the increase. There was racial violence. Dangerous international tension existed. We ran up record rates in divorce, drug addiction, and alcoholism. Millions of persons were suffering from chronic worry, hypertension, prejudice, guilt, hatred, and fear of failure.

About half the people in our hospitals had mental or emotional problems. Americans were spending more than a billion tax dollars every year to care for mental patients. For every person committed to a mental institution, a dozen were outside, groping in a half-real world. Ours was the age of anxiety. This was the age of the tranquilizer—we simply had given them more acceptable terms. We celebrated national mental health week. Our radio commercials and our billboards told us to bring our troubles out in the open. The world declared we should not be ashamed of mental confusion. These disturbed people were declared sick. Who can blame a sick person?

The social scientists were sure they could show the minister a better way after World War II. Three decades later, they are not so sure.

Today the word *sin* has all but disappeared. Many ministers have opted to embrace the social science route—especially in the counseling area. The Bible is a closed book to most people. The voice of the church grows weaker and weaker. We have become adept at helping people live with their sins. *Relief* is the popular word. Repentance of sin and cleansing is out. Tranquilizers and managing your urges are in.

Today's statistics make 1962 look like heaven. We are headed for the rocks with multitudes of ministers guiding the ship.

A Continuing Trend

More and more frequently pastors say to me, "Doc, I am thinking of leaving the ministry. How can I get in on what you are doing? You see, I have only studied theology and the Bible. How can I help people like you do?"

What a pity to hear a pastor refer to himself that way: "I *only* studied theology and the Bible."

Is it a pity? Or are you, with your training, the hope of the world? I see a trend among pastors who moved away from the Bible and toward the social sciences. Let me take a few moments to share my observations over the last fifty years.

> **Relief** *is the popular word. Repentance of sin and cleansing is out. Tranquilizers and managing your urges are in.*

If I were Satan, scanning the horizon in search of my competition, the person who would interfere most with my work would, of course, be the pastor. How would I neutralize his effectiveness? One way would be to talk him into turning away from his Bible and fill his mind instead with every possible kind of reading material. I would try to persuade the pastor that he needs to be knowledgeable in many fields, especially psychology, psychiatry, sociology, anthropology, economics, world affairs, social work, mental health, etc. Why, if I were Satan, would I recommend these fields to study? Because these writings are dominated by authors who reject God.

If I were Satan, I would attempt to persuade the pastor to put the Bible on trial—measure it against these other writings. If the Bible does not agree with them, then go along with these other writings. Better yet, just put the Bible aside. Above all, get our seminaries to study other books for guidance in life.

What are we to do with all the books on the market? Let me share my conclusion with you: Pure research in the human behavior field will lead you to a biblical principle. Further, most any author will have some views that coincide with Bible principles. On the other hand, the book may have many nonbiblical principles in it also. If there is one biblical principle, we tend to accept the whole book. If you must read these books, then let the book be on trial, not the Bible. It is good exercise, occasionally, to find out what your competition is saying. To discern what is biblical and nonbiblical assumes a thorough knowledge of the Bible.

> *Generally speaking, our nation has followed the leading of the social scientist, who has sought to produce a Godless, valueless, permissive society as the answer to our needs.*

Why put yourself in this position? Why not simply fill your head with the Word of God and declare it from the pulpit, the teaching podium, and across the desk? You need to apply the Bible to real life too!

Generally speaking, our nation has followed the leading of the social scientist, who has sought to produce a Godless, valueless, permissive society as the answer to our needs. We have tried it for a half century. Where has the trail led us? We are headed for the rocks, but we are not there yet.

The social sciences are changing the way we look at the nature of people. The social sciences are redefining sin. Anything from childish behavior to murder is some kind of syndrome or addiction.

A concerned mother asked me to observe her grade school age son. It seemed to me that he was an intelligent boy who could out-argue a confused single parent. Her son was on Ritalin and was diagnosed as "oppositional defiant disorder." The *Diagnostic and Statistical Manual for Mental Disorders (DSM)* describes this illness as a pattern of "nega- tivistic, defiant, disobedient, and hostile behavior toward authority fig- ures." Social scientists say, "These people are sick. They need therapy." A look at 2 Timothy 3:1–4 turns up the following words: *lovers of them- selves, disobedient, unforgiving, and headstrong.* This is behavior. These people need to be saved, cleansed, renewed, and empowered by the Holy Spirit. This is the minister's territory.

Another mother asked me to observe her son who was diagnosed with an "Attention Deficit Disorder." This boy, as I observed him, was a normal, rebellious child who was running wild because his parents were arguing with each other over many issues. Neither parent was able to focus on child training. Again, using the same Scripture, none of these people were sick. They were sinful. *Unthankful, unloving, without self-control,* and *haughty* were descriptive words that applied. This is sinful behavior. They need to be led to the truth by a faithful, loving minister.

Adultery has become sex addiction. The first edition of the *DSM* published in 1952 listed 112 mental disorders. *DSM* volume IV pub- lished in 1994 lists 374 mental disorders. That publication is filled with descriptions of sinful behavior redefined as sickness. Relief from this sickness is available. It is a relief to talk about one's problems. Listening to music, reading a book, exercise, and alcohol and drugs can have a calming effect. This world offers many sources that give relief.

The cure for these symptoms is to recognize them as sin—which is easily solved by coming to the Savior for help.

How would you answer these questions:

* Do you depend on observation or revelation for your guidance?
* Do you depend on self-control or regeneration?
* Do you depend on determination or transformation?
* Do you depend on training or yielding?

TIME TO CHANGE DIRECTION

Pastor, you can take back your territory! You can spring into the gap. You can take the helm. You can stand up once again, straight and tall and proud and say with the apostle Paul,

> Follow my example, as I follow the example of Christ.
>
> 1 COR. 11:1, NIV

The boat is still afloat. We can still change course. The first step is to put your faith in the right place.

> His divine power has given to us all things that pertain to life and godliness, through the knowledge of Him who called us by glory and virtue.
>
> 2 PET. 1:3

Use the Bible as God's Standard

Accurate assessment requires a standard measurement—the Bible. How do you justify the use of this standard? *Simple faith.* Consider the following verses as a basis for the assessment of a person's current condition:

> The LORD is my strength and my shield;
> My heart trusted in Him, and I am helped;
> Therefore my heart greatly rejoices,
> And with my song I will praise Him.
>
> PS. 28:7

> You will keep him in perfect peace,
> Whose mind is stayed on You,
> Because he trusts in You."
>
> ISA. 26:3

> Great peace have those who love Your law,
> And nothing causes them to stumble.
>
> PS. 119:165

> The work of righteousness will be peace,
> And the effect of righteousness, quietness and assurance
>   forever.
>
> ISA. 32:17

To sum up these verses, the person who is rightly related to God is the one who is cheerful, peaceful, quiet, righteous, and assured. These are a result of righteousness, not a prerequisite for righteousness. The following verses serve as a guide for assessing the cause of trouble:

He who covers his sins will not prosper,
But whoever confesses and forsakes them will have mercy.

Prov. 28:13

Behold, the LORD's hand is not shortened,
That it cannot save;
Nor His ear heavy,
That it cannot hear.
But your iniquities have separated you from your God;
And your sins have hidden His face from you,
So that He will not hear.

Isa. 59:1–2

"There is no peace,"
Says my God, "for the wicked."

Isa. 57:21

Acknowledge Sin

Here we find that the cause of distress in a person is sin, iniquity, wickedness. If you hope to get a person started on a program of self-development, it will be necessary to help him discover the sin, iniquity, and wickedness in his life. To do this, you must have a clear picture in your own mind of the content of sin. The basic definition of sin is in 1 John:

Whoever commits sin also commits lawlessness, and sin is lawlessness.

1 John 3:4

Other model verses are: 1 John 2:9; 5:17; James 2:9; 4:17; 1 Samuel 15:23; Colossians 3:5–9; Mark 7:15; Titus 3:1–4; Galatians 5:19.

In Psalm 15 there is a description of the person who shall never be moved. Such a person does the following:

- Walks blamelessly.
- Works righteousness.
- Speaks the truth from his heart.
- Has no slander on his tongue.
- Does no wrong toward his neighbor.

- Casts no slur against his neighbor.
- Despises a vile person.
- Honors them that fear God.
- Keeps his oath even when it hurts.
- Lends his money without interest.
- Does not take a bribe against the innocent.

In Galatians Paul described the works of the flesh and the Spirit:

THE FLESH	THE SPIRIT
Sexual Immorality	Love
Impurity	Joy
Debauchery	Peace
Idolatry	Patience
Witchcraft	Gentleness
Hatred	Kindness
Discord	Goodness
Jealousy	Faithfulness
Fits of Rage	Self-Control
Selfish Ambition	
Dissensions	
Factions	
Envying	
Drunkenness	
Orgies	

The Bible gives goals for our development, both long-range and immediate. We might consider the following immediate goals as found in God's Word:

If then you were raised with Christ, seek those things which are above, where Christ is, sitting at the right hand of God. Set your mind on things above, not on things on the earth.

COL. 3:1–2

But you, O man of God, flee these things and pursue righteousness, godliness, faith, love, patience, gentleness.

1 TIM. 6:11

> Casting down arguments and every high thing that exalts itself against the knowledge of God, bringing every thought into captivity to the obedience of Christ.
>
> 2 COR. 10:5

> "A new commandment I give to you, that you love one another; as I have loved you, that you also love one another."
>
> JOHN 13:34

Some long-range goals to be considered are the following:

> Now may the God of peace make you complete in every good work to do His will, working in you what is well pleasing in His sight, through Jesus Christ, to whom be glory forever and ever. Amen.
>
> HEB. 13:20–21

> Him we preach, warning every man and teaching every man in all wisdom, that we may present every man perfect in Christ Jesus.
>
> COL. 1:28

HOW TO REACH THE DESTINATION

We have looked at the present position. We have looked at the harbor, or the goal. Now we are faced with the question: How do we get there? There are two items we need to face:

1. Forgiveness which comes from God.
2. The surrender to the power of God if we are to reach our goal.

Forgiveness

There is a barrier that makes the confession of sin very difficult. Jesus referred to this barrier:

> And He said to them, "You are those who justify yourselves before men, but God knows your hearts. For what is highly esteemed among men is an abomination in the sight of God."
>
> LUKE 16:15

> And this is the condemnation, that the light has come into the world, and men loved darkness rather than light, because

their deeds were evil. For everyone practicing evil hates the light and does not come to the light, lest his deeds should be exposed.

JOHN 3:19–20

People will deny, suppress, repress, withdraw, and rationalize more readily than confess sins and repent. They prefer to find a reason for justifying their words, deeds, and emotions that are sinful rather than finding freedom from them. People prefer to change the circumstance or the other person rather than to seek a source of comfort in the circumstance or with the person.

People will deny, suppress, repress, withdraw, and rationalize more readily than confess sins and repent.

Accepting forgiveness for sin is also difficult. Many people insist that periods of depression, self-condemnation, sadness, remorse, or weeping are evidence of repentance. The simplicity of receiving forgiveness is hard to accept. The Scripture explains that godly sorrow leads to repentance:

Now I rejoice, not that you were made sorry, but that your sorrow led to repentance. For you were made sorry in a godly manner, that you might suffer loss from us in nothing. For godly sorrow produces repentance leading to salvation, not to be regretted; but the sorrow of the world produces death.

2 COR. 7:9–10

We want to correct our own ways. But only God can grant forgiveness.

Many people think that we must help God somehow. Confessing sin and seeking forgiveness goes counter to our natural way of doing things. We want to correct our own ways. But only God can grant forgiveness. When God knows that your heart is true to Him and ready to receive forgiveness, He will grant it. Only persons with a godly sorrow for their sin will be restored.

Surrender

The most difficult step of all is surrendering to the power of God. At first glance it would seem that to submit to the strength and power of God is something that everyone would gladly do.

Not that we are sufficient of ourselves to think of anything as being from ourselves, but our sufficiency is from God.

2 Cor. 3:5

"For whoever desires to save his life will lose it, but whoever loses his life for My sake will find it."

Matt. 16:25

On the contrary, people rebel against accepting their weakness or insufficiency. However, even if you acknowledge your inability to please God in the past, you tend to believe that since you understand the reason for past failures, you can now do better. People usually seek the answer to sinfulness in two ways: to justify past sins, and to retain confidence in themselves not to repeat past sins. People tend to resist the following course:

[God] who comforts us in all our tribulation, that we may be able to comfort those who are in any trouble, with the comfort with which we ourselves are comforted by God.

2 Cor. 1: 4

"But I say to you, love your enemies, bless those who curse you, do good to those who hate you, and pray for those who spitefully use you and persecute you."

Matt. 5:44

"But love your enemies, do good, and lend, hoping for nothing in return; and your reward will be great, and you will be sons of the Most High. For He is kind to the unthankful and evil."

Luke 6:35

To surrender to God is both a crisis and a daily process. There needs to be a clear, definite yielding of one's self completely to God, followed by day-by-day experience of that surrender. Note Paul's words:

Present yourselves to God as being alive from the dead, and your members as instruments of righteousness to God.

ROM. 6:13

Present your bodies a living sacrifice. . . . And do not be conformed to this world, but be transformed by the renewing of your mind, that you may prove what is that good and acceptable and perfect will of God.

ROM. 12:1–2

What do these passages mean? Simply this: that we are to give ourselves—body, mind, and soul—unreservedly to God. This is a matter of the will. How is this to be accomplished? Again, the Word of God is clear about this matter. It is by the work of the Holy Spirit. We must not only thank God for the indwelling of the Holy Spirit in our hearts (John 14:16–17; Rom. 8:9), but we must heed the command of the Word that we are to be "filled with the Spirit" (Eph. 5:18). Here is the secret of God's power—the Holy Spirit expressing Himself through us! He works in us only as we yield to Him.

It is one thing to make a broad, thoughtless statement that you will submit to God and another thing to surrender each detail of life to Him.

The yielded life is the life of peace. Yes, to surrender to God is to bring each circumstance of life to Him and receive from Him the strength to face it by His Spirit. It is one thing to make a broad, thoughtless statement that you will submit to God and another thing to surrender each detail of life to Him.

Personality development to me, then, is to help a person appreciate the fact of sin, the process involved in acknowledging sin, the problem of resisting sin, and the natural tendency to go it alone instead of submitting to the power of God. We tend to think of ourselves as adequate—that if we can understand, we can handle the problem by ourselves. Once this process becomes clear to the person so that he can use these steps in his own life, then your only job is to stand by and be available in case this person needs support at any step.

HENRY T. BLACKABY

The apostle Paul, in the midst of a very intellectually sophisticated world, warned God's people in Colosse:

> **See to it that no one carries you off as spoil or makes you yourselves captive by his so-called philosophy and intellectualism, and vain deceit (idle fancies and plain nonsense), following human tradition (men's ideas of the material rather than the spiritual) world, just crude notions following the rudimentary and elemental teachings of the universe, and disregarding [the teachings of] Christ (the Messiah). For in Him the whole fullness of Deity (the Godhead), continues to dwell in bodily form [giving complete expression of the divine nature].**

> COL. 2:8, AMP

THE VICTORIOUS CHRISTIAN LIFE
(Colossians 1:13–23)

God Has Done Great Things for Us (vv. 13–14)

1. God has delivered us from the kingdom of darkness. God "set us free" from darkness, real darkness (read also Matt. 4:12–17).
2. He has "conveyed us" into the Kingdom of the Son of His love. Now we live in a completely new realm of real life. He, now, is our way, our truth, and our life.
3. Through Christ, He gave us redemption through His blood—the forgiveness of sins. God provided and makes real in us a complete and full relationship with God. His resources for life are available to us (read also 2 Pet. 1:2–4; 2 Cor. 9:8).

Christ Is Now Our King (vv. 15–22)

1. Christ is the image of the invisible God. Christ is all of God, in us directly and personally and fully.
2. Christ is firstborn over all creation. He is the sample in His relation with God of what we are and are to become.
3. By Christ all things were created. Jesus brings to us all we need in life.

4. All things were created for Jesus Christ. He, in us, is the focus of all things.
5. Christ is before all things. He, who is now in us, was before anything else was. Therefore He is all we need.
6. In Christ all things consist. Everything "holds together" in Him, and He is holding our life and everything about it together.
7. Christ is the head of the body, the church. He, our King, is present in all His fullness right now in the midst of His people. Why, then, turn to the world when we have Him?
8. In all things Christ is to have the preeminence. It is purposed by God that we turn all things to Christ, and trust all things to Him.
9. All the fullness of the Godhead dwells in Christ. We, therefore, lack nothing that is needed for life, in its fullness.
10. By Christ, God reconciles all things to Himself. Anything out of harmony, or lacking in our life, Christ will bring it all to God for His fullness.
11. By Christ, God made peace and reconciled whether in heaven or on earth, by the blood of His flesh. Christ Himself is God's full provision to bring all of life into real and lasting peace and harmony with all God is purposing for us. He reconciled us to Himself to present us holy and blameless and above reproach in His sight.

The Christian Can Fully Experience the Riches of Christ (v. 23)

1. We can fully experience the riches of Christ if we continue in the faith. Our part is to confidently put our faith and trust in Him alone—in all things He has revealed in His Word to us by His Spirit.
2. We can fully experience the riches of Christ if we do not move away. Do not let the world deceive you to trust in anything other than Christ. The hope of the gospel is "confident expectation" in God's "good news" for every person. Bring His "good news" to everyone who crosses your life.
3. We can fully experience the riches of Christ if we hear Him. Now is where we make a real, crucial decision. You have "heard" from God. Do not be "moved away" from Him.

GOD'S RESOURCES FOR PASTORS

Oh, what a word to God's people today—especially to pastors, and through pastors in our broken and helpless world! Nobody in all of society, no professional of any kind, has such

- resources—to help all people;
- certainties—of true healing and wholeness;
- uniqueness—of opportunity to give real answers to real people in their real situation.

Jesus said to His disciples,

If you abide in My word, you are My disciples indeed. And you shall know the truth, and the truth shall make you free.

JOHN 8:31–32

Therefore if the Son makes you free, you shall be free indeed.

JOHN 8:36

Peace I leave with you, My peace I give to you; not as the world gives do I give to you. Let not your heart be troubled, neither let it be afraid.

JOHN 14:27

The world's ways, methods, abilities, and promises contrast vividly from those of God.

THE WORLD'S PROVISIONS	GOD'S PROVISIONS
temporary	lasting, permanent
inadequate	totally sufficient
provisional	unconditional
uncertain (little or no hope)	certain and full of hope
limited	unlimited
deceptive	true
tempting	satisfying
momentary	continuous
disappointing	fulfilling

If a pastor or leader will remain in God's Word, the Holy Spirit will bring him to the fullest confidence in God and His provision. God will also expose all that is deceptive and inadequate. Throughout Psalm 119, David gave certain witness to this contrast between the world and God's Word:

> **Turn away my eyes from looking at worthless things,**
> **And revive me in Your way.**
> **Establish Your word to Your servant,**
> **Who is devoted to fearing You.**
>
> PSALM 119:37–38

> **And I will walk at liberty,**
> **For I seek Your precepts.**
> **I will speak of Your testimonies also before kings,**
> **And will not be ashamed.**
>
> PS. 119:45–46

Pastor, stop right now! According to the Scriptures and life itself, does the world offer anything or do anything, greater than that which is yours in Jesus Christ? Does the world offer any guarantees? Are there any evidences of failure—utter failure?

I have spoken with hundreds of people who tried the world's promises and provisions and were helped temporarily only, but far worse, their hopes were dashed. They were like the New Testament woman who

> **had suffered many things from many physicians. She had**
> **spent all that she had and was no better, but rather grew**
> **worse.**
>
> MARK 5:26

Instinctively, she knew in her heart that Jesus could do for her what no one else could possibly do. She reached out her hand in faith and touched Him. She was instantly made whole. Then followed the incredible words from Jesus:

> **And He said to her, "Daughter, your faith has made you well.**
> **Go in peace, and be healed of your affliction."**
>
> MARK 5:34

Oh, how often I have been able to lead persons to put their faith in Jesus and what God promises are theirs in Jesus Christ. I have seen them made whole and leaving in peace. They have never again had to live with their affliction (whatever was sapping them of real life).

What the world cannot do, Christ will do. He will do what He promised. And when He does, the world will come to know Him.

Please, never exchange the world's ways (which are not real ways) for God's ways. It would be fatal to you and to those who come to you for help.

If a pastor or leader will remain in God's Word, the Holy Spirit will bring him to the fullest confidence in God and His provision.

PROCESS THE MESSAGE

1. Do you believe God has placed you where you are to lead others to hope? If so, how do you see your life as evidence of the hope of God?

2. Do you use God's Word as your standard?

3. According to the Scriptures and life itself, does the world offer anything or do anything greater than that which is yours in Jesus Christ?

4. Does the world offer any guarantees?

5. Are there any evidences of failure by the world to offer hope?

6. Do you know God's Word well enough to do biblical counseling?

THIRTEEN

Marks of Spiritual Leadership

> *"And when you saw that Nahash king of the Ammonites came against you, you said to me, 'No, but a king shall reign over us,' when the Lord your God was your king."*
>
> 1 SAMUEL 12:12
>
> *God Himself is the leader of His people. Israel's moment of greatest tragedy was when they asked for a king. . . . They wanted to be like the world around them and have a man to lead them. They rejected God as their Leader.*
>
> HENRY T. BLACKABY

HENRY T. BLACKABY

As I searched through the Scripture seeking to understand what God is looking for in the one He can use, I began to sense God does not look for "leaders," but rather for those

"whose heart is loyal to Him."

2 CHRON. 16:9

Certainly the supreme example of this is Jesus, of whom it was said,

And, once made perfect, he became the source of eternal salvation for all who obey him.

HEB. 5:9, NIV

Jesus was "shaped" or "made" by the Father into exactly the One He was looking for to redeem a lost world (Phil. 2:7; Isa. 53). He was Son and Servant to the Father. As a potter shapes the clay into the very vessel he needs to accomplish his purposes, so Jesus released His life to the Father and was made in the likeness of men. Even His soul was

> **an offering for sin.**
>
> ISA. 53:10

GOD IS THE LEADER

God Himself is the leader of His people. Israel's moment of greatest tragedy was when they asked for a king. After all that God had done— He had led them out of bondage into freedom, fed them when they were hungry, clothed them, gave them drink when they were thirsty— they turned to a man for their leader. What a huge step down! The people grew tired of doing things God's way and they said to Samuel,

> **"Look, you are old, and your sons do not walk in your ways. Now make us a king to judge us like all the nations." But the thing displeased Samuel when they said, "Give us a king to judge us." So Samuel prayed to the LORD.**
>
> 1 SAM. 8:5–6

Samuel immediately went to the right source for help. The Lord responded:

> **Heed the voice of the people in all that they say to you; for they have not rejected you, but they have rejected Me, that I should not reign over them.**
>
> 1 SAM. 8:7

They wanted to be like the world around them and have a man to lead them. They rejected God as their leader. Samuel saw with horror what they had done and said,

> **But you have today rejected your God, who Himself saved you from all your adversities and your tribulations; and you have said to Him, "No, set a king over us!"**
>
> 1 SAM. 10:19

Great suffering was about to come over the people of God. They were blind to all God had done for them in bringing them up out of Egypt. They had forsaken Him to serve other gods. God warned His people through His steward of what would happen should they reject God as their leader:

> **Now therefore, heed their voice. However, you shall solemnly forewarn them, and show them the behavior of the king who will reign over them.**
>
> 1 SAM. 8:9

Yet, being warned of their future

> **the people refused to obey the voice of Samuel; and they said, "No, but we will have a king over us, that we also may be like all the nations, and that our king may judge us and go out before us and fight our battles."**
>
> 1 SAM. 8:19–20

Then God described the behavior of their future earthly king:

> **He will take your sons and appoint them for his own chariots and to be his horsemen, and some will run before his chariots. He will appoint captains over his thousands and captains over his fifties, will set some to plow his ground and reap his harvest, and some to make his weapons of war and equipment for his chariots. He will take your daughters to be perfumers, cooks, and bakers. And he will take the best of your fields, your vineyards, and your olive groves, and give them to his servants. He will take a tenth of your grain and your vintage, and give it to his officers and servants. And he will take your male servants, your female servants, your finest young men, and your donkeys, and put them to his work. He will take a tenth of your sheep. And you will be his servants.**
>
> 1 SAM. 8:11–17

It is true that God places human leaders as stewards and managers over His people. However, a man can become the wrong kind of leader. The greatness of having God as your leader is that He will never become something less than the very best.

In the midst of His people God looks for one (or more) "whose heart is loyal to Him" so He can prove Himself strong on their behalf. This servant is a "worker together with God" (2 Cor. 6:1). But among *His* people *He* is always their leader.

THE LORD JESUS AS LEADER

> *The greatness of having God as your leader is that He will never become something less than the very best.*

In the New Testament God placed His Son, our Lord Jesus, to be the leader over His people. A pastor is His servant to guide His people to serve and follow Him. The people are *God's*; the pastor is a *steward* of what is God's.

The world is doing everything possible to provide leadership and direction for countries, states, corporations, clubs, and organizations. Since the world does not acknowledge God, their leaders are just substitutes for the One who alone can provide true leadership.

Thus, from a human perspective these persons are leaders. But from God's perspective, they are stewards or managers of *His* possession. He alone is our God, and we are His people. God chooses, calls, or appoints someone to guide His people to Him. As servants we are to submit to Him, obey Him, and follow Him.

The clearest picture of this servant relationship to God is Jesus. The most profound example of Jesus' relationship with His Father in the midst of His people is John 17. Here is a Servant Steward at his best.

It would do well for us to remember Jesus' words to His disciples:

> **A disciple is not above his teacher, nor a servant above his master. It is enough for a disciple that he be like his teacher, and a servant like his master.**
>
> MATT. 10:24–25

MARKS OF SPIRITUAL LEADERS

God not only chooses His servants but also rejects some people to guide His people. Notice the wording carefully of that decisive moment in the life of God's people when God rejected Saul, and chose David:

> **And Samuel said to Saul, "You have done foolishly. You have not kept the commandment of the LORD your God, which He commanded you. For now the LORD would have established your kingdom over Israel forever. But now your kingdom shall not continue. The LORD has sought for Himself a man after His own heart, and the LORD has commanded him to be commander over His people, because you have not kept what the LORD commanded you."**
>
> 1 SAM. 13:13–14

Preeminently the Lord looks for one whose heart "is loyal to Him" (2 Chron. 16:9). This is a man after God's own heart! Character precedes assignment, determines assignment, and maintains assignment. The world may look at the skills, success, and personality, but these are merely outward appearance. God looks on the heart (1 Sam. 16:7). And the Scripture adds,

> *A pastor is His servant to guide His people to serve and follow Him.*

> **And the Spirit of the Lord came upon David from that day forward.**
>
> 1 SAM. 16:13

From that day of God's choosing, David entered into a progressively intimate relationship with God, and with God's people.

> **He also chose David His servant,**
> **And took him from the sheepfolds;**
> **From following the ewes that had young He brought him,**
> **To shepherd Jacob His people,**
> **And Israel His inheritance.**
> **So he shepherded them according to the integrity of his heart,**
> **And guided them by the skillfulness of his hands.**
>
> PS. 78:70–72

John 17 looks at spiritual leadership from two perspectives: (1) from God's perspective and activity; and (2) from man's perspective on what

God does to show those He has chosen to guide His people. Jesus, of course, is our ideal spiritual leader. He carries two crucial relationships:

1. His relationship to His Father, who sent Him and gave Him His people to provide for and to guide into all the purposes God had for them.
2. His relationship to those God gave Him. They were the Father's, and He gave them to His Son (John 17:6–8).

John 17 is Jesus' great prayer to the Father at the close of His life—probably just before Gethsemane and the crucifixion. It is a sensitive, focused summary of His faithful stewardship over those God had given Him. Today Christ indwells every leader God calls, guiding and enabling them to function with God's people as He did in the days of His flesh.

What many today are looking for in a "Spiritual Leader" is seen so clearly in the relationship Jesus had to His disciples as a steward of His Father.

What does one appointed by God to lead His people do? How does he function with the Father to lead the people? It is crucial to look at John 17 carefully as a plumb line for your leadership "style."

Mark #1: A Servant Leader's Goal:

To Let Jesus Glorify the Father Through Him

> **Jesus spoke these words, lifted up His eyes to heaven, and said: "Father, the hour has come. Glorify Your Son, that Your Son also may glorify You."**
>
> JOHN 17:1

Jesus knew the cross was near. He also knew "God was in Christ reconciling a world to Himself" (2 Cor. 5:19). He asked the Father to glorify Him; that is, reveal in and through Him exactly who Jesus was by vindicating His life before a watching world. In fully obeying the Father, Jesus' life revealed once and for all the loving nature and work of the Father in bringing His salvation to a lost and hell-bound world. If the Father revealed His Son, the son would thoroughly reveal the Father. Jesus' goal was to reveal fully His Father to our world.

The first priority of a spiritual leader is to live in union with God, fully loving and obeying Him in all moments, so that our Lord will be glorified in him or her. The world must have an accurate, unchanged encounter with Jesus as He really is, by watching and encountering our lives.

Mark #2: A Servant Leader's Credentials:

Given by God, Not Men

> **"As You have given Him authority over all flesh, that He should give eternal life to as many as You have given Him."**
>
> JOHN 17:2

No man can grant "spiritual credentials" for a spiritual leader. These come from God alone. What the Father granted to Jesus, the Father was present to bring about in and through Jesus' life (John 8:25–30; 14:10). The "credentials" of a spiritual leader is the presence of God, at all points authenticating His servant. God did this to Moses, the judges, the prophets—and His own Son. The authority exercised by Jesus, in His teaching, preaching, and healing, was God's open mark to a watching world. This is granted to every true spiritual leader, by God alone. A spiritual leader never has to persuade or pressure God's people. The obvious presence of God is open for all to see—and they respond.

Jesus gave to His disciples "authority" to God in His name (Matt. 10:1ff.). He gave them "the keys of the kingdom of heaven" (Matt. 16:19). And Paul said God made us "ambassadors for Christ" (2 Cor. 5:20).

This is as real today as it ever was. To only have the "authority of men" and not be "endued with power from on high" is to put all the people of God in jeopardy, as well as God's purpose to redeem. Those God uses have His authority revealed in and through their lives.

Mark #3: A Servant Leader's Assignment:

To Give Eternal Life to Those Entrusted to His Care

A true spiritual leader has an assignment. Jesus indicated what the authority given to Him was for:

> **That He should give eternal life to as many as You have given Him.**
>
> JOHN 17:2

Eternal life is not merely the assurance that one is going to heaven when he or she dies. Rather, Jesus defined eternal life clearly:

> **This is eternal life, that they may know You, the only true God, and Jesus Christ whom You have sent.**
>
> JOHN 17:3

To "know" is a progressive, experiential relationship with God—and His Son—to perceive, understand, and experience Him more intimately and personally. This is exactly what Jesus did—He assured them that if they had known and seen Him (Jesus), they had known and seen the Father (John 14:9–11).

As a spiritual leader, this was Jesus' assignment to His disciples: to bring them to experience the fullness of God.

> **"Teaching them to observe all things that I have commanded you."**
>
> MATT. 28:20

Paul's assignment was to "present every person perfect [complete] in Christ" (Col. 1:27–29), and he prayed that God's people would be "filled with all the fullness of God" (Eph. 3:16–19).

It would be very helpful to read through the New Testament and make a list of all the commands of Jesus. Then begin to teach the people of God to practice everything you find.

Mark #4: A Servant Leader's Passion:

To Finish His God-Given Work

> **"I have glorified You on the earth. I have finished the work which You have given Me to do."**
>
> JOHN 17:4

Certainly Jesus' major work was His involvement with the Father in redemption. But included in God's "great salvation" was Jesus' assignment with the disciples, whom the Father had given Him. This prayer reveals the extensiveness of His commitment in the lives of the disciples, preparing them and keeping them for the Father's purpose to redeem the rest of the world. So, when Jesus said, "I have finished the work You gave me to do," He concluded three and a half years of intensive obedience to the Father's purposes and instructions concerning the disciples. The disciples were the focus of His ministry. For He knew that on the lives of these disciples would rest the Father's activity to save a world.

This is always true for those to whom God entrusts His own. For on these will rest the redemption of the world. The unfolding of what was involved in this stewardship is seen in the rest of Jesus' prayer, but it is obvious, His passion was "to finish the work" God had purposed for Him to do with the disciples.

Mark #5: A Servant Leader's Focus:

To Manifest the Father's Name

> **"I have manifested Your name to the men whom You have given Me out of the world. They were Yours, You gave them to Me, and they have kept Your word."**
>
> JOHN 17:6

God's name is His character. All the "I Am's" revealed God to His people over the centuries. Jesus' focus was to guide the disciples into the fullest understanding and experience of the Father. They knew the Father's love—because Jesus let God love them through Him. Jesus manifested the Father's faithfulness, mercy, power, sovereignty, and presence by faithfully living "in union with" the Father, so the disciples were face to face with God. It was crucial for the disciples to know the Father and respond to Him, for world redemption would be greatly affected.

No leader can possibly lead where he has not been or share what he has not knowingly experienced. The disciples came to know God by observing and practicing everything Jesus commanded. And this is how those we lead will come to know the Father and His Son.

Mark #6: A Servant Leader's Stewardship:

Those God Entrusted to Him

> **"They were Yours, You gave them to Me, and they have kept Your word."**
>
> JOHN 17:6B

Jesus did not choose the disciples—they were given to Him by the Father. He was therefore a steward of God's "treasure" (Exod. 19). Jesus cared for them intensely and faithfully; *they* were His ministry. He did not "use" them but related to them as directed by the Father.

Likewise, "God has set the members, each one of them, in the body [church] just as He pleased" (1 Cor. 12:18). Those He adds are His, and He has entrusted them to us. We must not use them for our purposes and goals, but see them as our ministry!

Mark #7: A Servant Leader's Resources:

All God Has Given to Him, He Gives to the Disciples

> **"Now they have known that all things which You have given Me are from You."**
>
> JOHN 17:7

Three and a half years with Jesus provided the disciples with overwhelming evidence of all God had given to Christ—authority, power, words, the fullness of His Spirit, love—and they knew that it was clearly from God.

For a spiritual leader to lead God's people effectively, there must be clear evidence of a Spirit-filled life, thorough immersion in God's Word, the manifest presence of Christ (John 14:21), the wisdom of God, the love of God, and the power of God (Acts 1:8).

Do those you lead know the resources of God are indeed present in and through your life? If not, why not?

Mark #8: A Servant Leader's Teacher's Heart:

That the Disciples May Learn

> **"For I have given to them the words which You have given Me; and they have received them, and have known surely that I came forth from You; and they have believed that You sent Me."**
>
> JOHN 17:8

Jesus received from the Father His words and gave them to the disciples. The disciples received them and came to know by experience and believe that Jesus was sent from the Father. This threefold combination of (1) receiving, (2) knowing, and (3) believing Him was the essence of what God had purposed for the disciples. On this, Jesus would

- build His church (Matt. 16:18);
- give them the keys to His kingdom (Matt. 16:19);

- commission them to take His gospel to all people (Matt. 28:19–20);
- fill them with His Spirit to enable them to accomplish it all (Acts 1:8).

Jesus taught the disciples for two and a half years before He had their hearts confirmed that He was the Christ! Every pastor or leader *must* have a passion to teach God's people *until* they are thoroughly convinced by God who Jesus is. Everything rests on this. To fail here is to fail in God's plan to redeem the world.

Mark #9: A Servant Leader's Prayer Focus:

Not the World but Those Entrusted to Him

> **"I pray for them. I do not pray for the world but for those whom You have given Me, for they are Yours."**
>
> JOHN 17:9

Again and again the Bible mentions Jesus leaving the multitudes, taking the disciples with Him so He could teach them. When He knew Satan had requested to sift them as wheat, He assured them: "I have prayed for you" (Luke 22:31–32). Paul assured the Romans that Christ "makes intercession for us" (Rom. 8:34). Paul knew, as did Jesus, that the redemption of the world depended on God's people as disciples.

You *must* focus on God's people as your major passion in prayer. Faithful intercession for those entrusted to you is crucial. It is a mark of a spiritual leader whose heart has been shaped by God.

This is why Peter urged,

> **But as He who called you is holy, you also be holy in all your conduct, because it is written, "Be holy, for I am holy."**
>
> 1 PET. 1:15–16

Mark #10: A Servant Leader's Reputation:

The Lives of His Disciples

> **"And all Mine are Yours, and Yours are Mine, and I am glorified in them."**
>
> JOHN 17:10

This is one of the most amazing statements of Jesus: "I am glorified in them." The lives of the disciples—examples of what Jesus taught—and His very life *in them* was what "glorified" Jesus. It was not enough that he gave them "head knowledge." Their lives must manifest the full life of Christ their Lord to a watching world. As the Father was glorified in the Son, so Christ would be glorified in His disciples.

This is crucial: A leader is only as effective as the lives of those he is leading. The people we lead are a reflection (manifestation) of our life. A spiritual leader produces spiritual followers.

> **And the things that you have heard from me among many witnesses, commit these to faithful men who will be able to teach others also.**
>
> 2 TIM. 2:2

Mark #11: A Servant Leader's Investment:

Rests in His Disciples' Faithfulness

> **"Now I am no longer in the world, but these are in the world, and I come to You."**
>
> JOHN 17:11A

Jesus was soon to return to the Father. These disciples would remain. The implementing of what God accomplished in Christ to redeem a world would now rest with the disciples.

A spiritual leader must give very close attention to those entrusted to him. After the leader is gone, his work (God's work) will rest with those he led. To ensure the continuation of God's redemptive work, Jesus did two things: (1) invested thoroughly in the disciples the Father gave Him; and (2) prayed that God would do in them what He had done in Jesus. A wise spiritual leader will (1) invest carefully and purposefully in those entrusted to Him; (2) pray constantly for the Father to work in them.

Mark #12: A Servant Leader's Success:

To Ensure That Each Finishes Well

> **"Holy Father, keep through Your name those whom You have given Me, that they may be one as We are."**
>
> JOHN 17:11B

In John 6:39, Jesus said,

> **This is the will of the Father who sent Me, that of all He has given Me I should lose nothing, but should raise it up at the last day.**

Now Jesus is returning to the Father and asks Him to "keep through Your name those whom You have given Me." All the Father is, as Jesus revealed Him to the disciples, would secure them permanently "in Christ," so the fullness of God and His purposes would be expressed and accomplished in and through them.

A spiritual leader must commit to God every person God has entrusted to him—bringing each person to the fullest relationship to the Father, His Son, and His Spirit. Each must purposefully respond to all of God's activity, to ensure that His eternal purposes for them will be secured.

Many today are beginning well, and running well, but not finishing the race. A spiritual leader will ensure that each finishes well!

Mark #13: A Servant Leader's Joy:

His Disciples

> **"That they may be one as We are."**
>> JOHN 17:11B

> **"That they may have My joy fulfilled in themselves."**
>> JOHN 17:13B

Completeness of joy in Jesus is based on faith:

> **"Believe Me that I am in the Father and the Father in Me. . . ."**
>> JOHN 14:11

> **and "abide in My love."**
>> JOHN 15:9

> **"These things I have spoken to you, that My joy may remain in you, and that your joy may be full."**
>> JOHN 15:11

Jesus' joy was His relationship with His Father—and that His disciples would be in this same relationship so that they may be as one.

A true spiritual leader's joy is in the "oneness" with his people. One with each other because they are "one" with their Lord. The corporate life of God's people is a reflection of their corporate and personal relationship with their one Lord.

A spiritual leader will always work and pray to this end. Jesus had said this oneness in love would be the distinguishing mark to the world that they were His disciples (John 13:34–35).

Mark #14: A Servant Leader's Strategy:

To Give His Disciples God's Word

> **"I have given them Your word."**
>
> JOHN 17:14A

Jesus had just said,

> **I have called you friends, for all things that I heard from My Father I have made known to you.**
>
> JOHN 15:15B

He had assured them,

> **I do not speak on My own authority; but the Father who dwells in Me does the works.**
>
> JOHN 14:10B

If Jesus had a "strategy" for the disciples' lives, it was to receive the words of the Father for them, and share them faithfully. God's Word for the disciples was their very life (Deut. 32:46–47; John 6:63).

A spiritual leader knows it is not his words or thoughts God's people need. God is the One who has a word and purpose for each of His people. A spiritual leader, like Jesus, receives from the Father and shares what he hears with God's people—daily.

Mark #15: A Servant Leader's Burden:

The World's Hatred

> **"And the world has hated them because they are not of the world, just as I am not of the world."**
>
> JOHN 17:14B

Jesus knew the full-blown hatred of the world toward Him. He also knew if the disciples followed Him, the world would hate them also. Light and darkness do not remain together. No one can serve two masters. The very presence of God and His Word create decision! A heart not open to God will reject Him and His Word, with ever-increasing violence. Jesus knew this would be a very real part of the disciples' lives, and He sought to prepare them and interceded for them.

A true spiritual leader knows that his own life will come in conflict with sin and the flesh and the devil. He first gains victory in his own life, then seeks to prepare God's people for the opposition and pain they will experience when they become true and passionate followers of Jesus Christ. In addition, he makes intercession for them diligently. Often, the great burden of a spiritual leader will be "the shepherd's care for his flock"—even to the laying down of his life for them (John 10:11; Eph. 5:25–27; 1 John 3:16).

A burdened heart is characteristic of a true spiritual leader. He carries the hurts of God's people.

Mark #16: A Servant Leader's Prayer:

To Be Kept from the Evil One

> **"I do not pray that You should take them out of the world, but that You should keep them from the evil one."**
>
> **JOHN 17:15B**

As the Father "kept Jesus" from the evil one, so Jesus asks the Father to do this in His disciples. He did not pray for the Father to keep the evil one from them—but them from the evil one.

First, that their "faith should not fail" (Luke 22:31–32).

Second, that all God's provision (armor of God, Eph. 6:10–19) would be in place in each one. Jesus prepared the disciples with teaching (truth) that would free them (John 8:31–32, 36). The more they knew their God, the more they could and would resist the enemy. Jesus modeled this in His own life and equipped the disciples to resist.

Every spiritual leader can be fully prepared to resist the enemy by the enabling provisions of God's presence, and will teach and enable God's people to respond to His provisions for them. He prays not for the enemy to be kept from them, but they from the enemy (Matt. 6:13).

Mark #17: A Servant Leader's Assurance:

That the Father Will Sanctify Those Entrusted to His Care

> **"Sanctify them by Your truth. Your word is truth."**
>
> JOHN 17:17

Jesus had absolute confidence in His Father and the Father's activity in the disciples. Jesus knew what He Himself could do and what only the Father could do. "Sanctifying" them (i.e., setting them apart for Himself as holy) was the work of the Father. Jesus knew that the Father did this by His word. So Jesus shared all the words of His Father with the disciples, knowing

- his word (truth) was their life;
- the Father was present, helping the disciples hear, understand, and obey;
- his word, if obeyed, would bring God's full presence and activity in each disciple, bringing them freedom, abundant life, and victory (Matt. 16:17–19).

Every spiritual leader knows that a word from God brings life to every child of God who

- comes to Him;
- hears;
- obeys (Luke 6:46ff.).

Isaiah said that when God speaks, His word never "returns void" but accomplishes everything it was sent to do (Isa. 55:8–13).

A spiritual leader has unswerving confidence in the words of God. He knows and hears them clearly and faithfully and shares them fully and confidently with God's people. He is confident that God Himself is at work in each to set them apart for Himself.

Mark #18: A Servant Leader's Mandate:

To Send His Disciples into the World as He Was Sent by the Father

> **"As You sent Me into the world, I also have sent them into the world."**
>
> JOHN 17:18

All the life of Jesus with His disciples came down to their being sent into the world, as He was sent into the world. This was the Father's will and purpose! The Father had entrusted the disciples to Jesus. Then the Father told Jesus what to tell them, to prepare them for God's plan to redeem a world through them.

A spiritual leader must know fully the "sending" of the Father in his own life. Only then can he share that this process in the lives of those entrusted to him. He must

- prepare them, by diligent, thorough teaching and enabling;
- prepare them by an intimate, real relationship with God;
- know when the Father has completed their equipping (Matt. 10; 16:15–27).
- faithfully "send them into the world"—as the Father has sent the leader.

Mark #19: A Servant Leader's Sensitivity:

To Sanctify Himself that Those Entrusted to Him Might Be Sanctified by the Truth

> **"And for their sakes I sanctify Myself, that they also may be sanctified by the truth."**
>
> **JOHN 17:19**

At this very point seems to rest God's redemptive plan for the world: His children are "sanctified" by His truth—sent into the world as Jesus was. Jesus knew this. So He said to the Father, "For *their* sakes, I sanctify Myself, *that* they also may be sanctified" (my emphasis).

All that the disciples were to become, He exemplified in His own life! By being with Jesus, they knew

- the Father had sent Him into the world;
- the Holy Spirit had filled Him;
- the Father's Word directed Him;
- God was with Him;
- He always pleased (obeyed) the Father;
- God redeemed (saved) people through Him;
- nothing deterred Him;
- He was "complete" (Heb. 5:9) in every way.

A spiritual leader, above all else, is a living pattern and expression of all he is seeking for God's people. The people we lead will rise no higher in the will of God than we as their spiritual leader.

The whole purpose of God for His people may stall right here—or may be powerful and explosive, as seen in the early church in the Book of Acts. This is why the apostles said,

> **But we will give ourselves continually to prayer and to the ministry of the word.**
>
> ACTS 6:4

Mark #20: The Servant Leader's Long-Term Look:

To Sanctify All Who Would Believe the Word to the End of Time

> **"I do not pray for these alone, but also for those who will believe in Me through their word."**
>
> JOHN 17:20

Jesus' intense and sensitive labor of love with His disciples was not for them alone—but for all who would believe through them, to the end of time. So much more was at stake than just the disciples!

So it is with every true spiritual leader. He does not only labor for those entrusted to his care—but has in mind the endless multitude whose lives will be affected because he faithfully trained and equipped those given to him. Some will become missionaries and Christian workers in the marketplaces of the world. Each will be prepared and commissioned by God, as Jesus was.

Paul was aware of the far-reaching impact of his efforts:

> **For we are to God the fragrance of Christ among those who are being saved and among those who are perishing.**
>
> 2 COR. 2:15

> **Now thanks be to God who always leads us in triumph in Christ, and through us diffuses the fragrance of His knowledge in every place.**
>
> 2 COR. 2:14

A spiritual leader has this "long look" in all those entrusted to him.

Mark #21: A Servant Leader's Kingdom View:

That They May Be One

> **"That they all may be one, as You, Father, are in Me, and I in You; that they also may be one in Us, that the world may believe that You sent Me."**
>
> JOHN 17:21

God's Plan:
God was "in Christ"
Christ was "in God"
Christ was "in the disciples"
The disciples were "in Christ"
The world would believe

Jesus was fully responsive to the Father, so the Father was fully present in His Son to accomplish His purpose to redeem. Christ would be fully in the disciples as they were fully "in Him" (responsive to Him as Lord). The Father, in Christ, and Christ in the disciples would bring a world to believe.

Likewise, "all the fullness of God" is present in Christ in a leader of God's people (Eph. 3:19; Col. 2:9). As that leader releases his life in those entrusted to him, that same fullness becomes real and personal in God's people. In such people, indwelt by God's fullness in Christ, a world could believe God sent His Son to redeem them.

Mark #22: A Servant Leader's Gift:

Giving Glory to His Disciples

> **"And the glory which You gave Me I have given them, that they may be one just as We are one."**
>
> JOHN 17:22

What an enabling for a spiritual leader! The glory given to Jesus— given to His disciples! The glory is the full presence of God expressed openly in and through Jesus' life. All that the Father was to Jesus He imparted to His disciples. They would need God's presence in and through them as they went into their world.

It is eminently true that a leader cannot share what he does not have. There must be a "fullness of God" in a spiritual leader for God's people to share in His fullness. Some have observed that the "fullness of God" is *caught* more than just *taught*.

A spiritual leader must take seriously this pattern by Jesus. The "glory" given to the leader must be given to those in his care through his prayer life, his faith, his power, his love, and his Christlikeness. God's people long to see in their leader the life they long for themselves.

Mark #23: A Servant Leader's Union:

Union with God in Christ for Himself and His People

> **"I in them, and You in Me; that they may be made perfect in one, and that the world may know that You have sent Me, and have loved them as You have loved Me."**
>
> JOHN 17:23

The intensity of these words cannot be underestimated! "I in them" and "You [God] in Me."

> **For in Him dwells all the fullness of the Godhead bodily.**
>
> COL. 2:9

This was Paul's passion: "To know Him"—and to lead all God's people into this same relationship! This was the focus of nearly all Paul's prayers. And this was the heartcry of Jesus for His disciples.

When this fullness is real in the corporate life of God's people, "the world may know that You have sent Me, and have loved them as You have loved Me."

Here is where a true spiritual leader stays and meditates thoroughly, and measures his leadership and stewardship of God's people. Here is God's plan and purpose and strategy to bring a lost world to Himself: God, in Christ, in His people—bringing union with His Fullness so a world will know and believe:

- God sent Jesus;
- God loves His people as He loves His Son;
- This relationship is available to all who will believe.

A spiritual leader will not rest, or be satisfied, until all of God's purpose is being lived out in his life and the lives of those entrusted to him.

To them God willed to make known what are the riches of the glory of this mystery among the Gentiles: which is Christ in you, the hope of glory. Him we preach, warning every man and teaching every man in all wisdom, that we may present every man perfect in Christ Jesus. To this end I also labor, striving according to His working which works in me mightily.

COL. 1:27–29

Mark #24: A Servant Leader's Desire:

To Lead His People to the Fullest Possible Relationship with God and His Son

"Father, I desire that they also whom You gave Me may be with Me where I am, that they may behold My glory which You have given Me; for You loved Me before the foundation of the world."

JOHN 17:24

Jesus was fully "bonded" in love to the disciples given to Him by His Father. They were loved by the Father and therefore loved by Jesus. He wanted them

- To be with Him;
- To behold His glory;
- To see the love of God for Him from before the foundation of the world.

The leader must not only lead, but love God's people. He begins with his own relationship with God—deep, personal, real, and complete. God's people must first "see" this in their leader and desire this for themselves.

A spiritual leader must eagerly strive to be God's servant, experiencing God's fullness. He does not lead his people primarily into "church growth"—buildings and activities—but to the fullest relationship possible with God and His Son (Eph. 3:14–21).

Mark #25: A Servant Leader's Satisfaction:

To Know that Those Entrusted to Him Have Come to Know the Father

> **"O righteous Father! The world has not known You, but I
> have known You; and these have known that You sent Me."**
>
> JOHN 17:25

As Jesus began to close His prayer concerning His disciples, He expressed His deepest satisfaction.

His heart for the disciples was for them to know the Father, and how and why the Father sent His Son for them, and through them to a world who does not know Him.

A spiritual leader has this also as his deep satisfaction—those entrusted to him by God have come to know Him as God purposed, and now the Father can "send them into the world" with God's good news for a lost world.

All that follows in the Book of Acts verifies Jesus' heart satisfaction in this prayer. All that happens in God's people in their world verifies and authenticates a spiritual leader's life and ministry.

Mark #26: A Servant Leader's Completeness:

That the Disciples Be Loved by the Same Love the Father Expressed to Jesus

> **"And I have declared to them Your name, and will declare it,
> that the love with which You loved Me may be in them, and I
> in them."**
>
> JOHN 17:26

This last verse seems to sum up the whole prayer of Jesus. The Father had entrusted to Him twelve men and those who would believe through them. The Father had loved His Son unconditionally and fully, as the Father was "in Christ reconciling the world to Himself" (2 Cor. 5:19). Now Christ would be in the disciples as the Father was in Him, continuing to reconcile a world to Himself.

The whole life of Jesus rested in and was an expression of the Father's love! Here Jesus wrapped it all up and asked the Father to love these disciples with this same love—love that would "compel" them (2 Cor. 5:14).

A spiritual leader is one who is immersed in the Love of God, the love of Christ, and the love of the Holy Spirit, which compels, controls, motivates, initiates, guides, and leads him in all his relationship with God's people entrusted to him. Literally the love of Christ touches everyone around him, and his greatest desire is to "present everyone perfect in Christ." This he accomplishes, just like Jesus did, "according to His working which works in [him] mightily" (Col. 1:28–29).

A spiritual leader does not rest until every person in his care comes

> **to the unity of the faith and of the knowledge of the Son of God, to a perfect man, to the measure of the stature of the fullness of Christ.**
>
> EPH. 4:13

This is our goal! This is God's goal. This is God's "strategy" for redeeming a lost world—everywhere, at all times. Take time to compare the way you lead the people God gave you with how our Lord Jesus Christ led His disciples. May Christ's pattern be so in each of us who have been called to be a spiritual leader of God's people.

PROCESS THE MESSAGE

1. Have you looked to the world for a "style" of leadership? What is the latest book you may have turned to for direction?

2. How would you describe to someone the difference between having a "vision" for the church versus having "God's vision" for the church?

3. When was the last time you studied the life of Jesus as your style of leadership?

4. How would you explain to the church the difference between "God being the leader" and looking to a "person for a leader"?

5. How does your "method" or "style" line up to Jesus' style illustrated in John 17?

MARKS OF A SERVANT LEADER (JOHN 17)

1	A Servant Leader's Goal — To let Jesus glorify the Father through him	17:1
2	A Servant Leader's Credentials — Given by God, not men	17:2
3	A Servant Leader's Assignment — To give Eternal Life to those entrusted to his care	17:2
4	A Servant Leader's Passion — To finish his God-given work	17:4
5	A Servant Leader's Focus — To manifest the Father's name	17:6
6	A Servant Leader's Stewardship — Those God entrusted to him	17:6
7	A Servant Leader's Resources — All God has given him, he gives to the disciples	17:7
8	A Servant Leader's Teacher's Heart — That the disciples may learn who Jesus is	17:8
9	A Servant Leader's Prayer Focus — Not the world but those entrusted to him	17:9
10	A Servant Leader's Reputation — The lives of his disciples	17:10
11	A Servant Leader's Investment — Rests in his disciples' faithfulness	17:11a
12	A Servant Leader's Success — To ensure that each finishes well	17:11b
13	A Servant Leader's Joy — His disciples	17:13
14	A Servant Leader's Strategy — To give his disciples God's Word	17:14a
15	A Servant Leader's Burden — The world's hatred	17:15
16	A Servant Leader's Prayer — To be kept from the evil one	17:15b
17	A Servant Leader's Assurance — That the Father will sanctify those entrusted to his care	17:17-19
18	A Servant Leader's Mandate — To send his disciples into the world as he was sent by the Father	17:18
19	A Servant Leader's Sensitivity — To sanctify himself that those entrusted to him might be sanctified by the truth	17:19
20	A Servant Leader's Long-term Look — To sanctify all who would believe the Word to the end of time	17:20, 22-23
21	A Servant Leader's Kingdom View — That they may be one	17:21
22	A Servant Leader's Gift — Giving glory to his disciples	17:22
23	A Servant Leader's Union — Union with God in Christ for himself and his people	17:23
24	A Servant Leader's Desire — To lead his people to the fullest possible relationship with God and His Son	17:24a
25	A Servant Leader's Satisfaction — To know that those entrusted to him have come to know the Father	17:25
26	A Servant Leader's Completeness — That the disciples be loved by the same love the Father expressed to Jesus	17:26

Recommended Reading
for Pastors and Leaders

Books by These Authors

Blackaby, Henry T. *What the Spirit Is Saying to the Churches*. Atlanta: Home Mission Board, 1988.

———. *Lift High the Torch*. Nashville: Convention Press, 1992.

———. *Called and Accountable*. Birmingham: Woman's Missionary Union, 1992.

Blackaby, Henry T. and Claude V. King. *Experiencing God: Knowing & Doing the Will of God*. Nashville: LifeWay Press, 1990. (Interactive workbook)

———. *Experiencing God: How to Live the Full Adventure of Knowing and Doing the Will of God*. Broadman & Holman, 1994. (Trade book)

———. *Fresh Encounter: God's Pattern for Revival and Spiritual Awakening*. Nashville: LifeWay Press, 1993. (Interactive workbook).

———. *Fresh Encounter: Experiencing God through Prayer, Humility, and a Heart-felt Desire to Know Him*. Nashville: Broadman & Holman, 1996. (Trade book)

Brandt, Henry. *Breaking Free from the Bondage of Sin*. Eugene, Oreg., 1994. Available through Life Change, 147 Hayes Circle, Rex, GA 30273.

Brandt, Henry and Kerry L. Skinner. *The Heart of the Problem: A Prescription for a Deeper Experience with God*. Nashville: Broadman & Holman, 1995. (Interactive workbook)

_____. *The Heart of the Problem*. Nashville: Broadman & Holman, 1996. (Trade book)

_____. *The Word for the Wise: Making the Scripture the Heart of Your Counseling Ministry*. Professional Development Books. Nashville: Broadman & Holman, 1995.

The Pastor/Leader and His Life

Blackaby, Henry T. and Claude V. King. *Experiencing God: Knowing and Doing the Will of God*. Nashville: LifeWay Press, 1990. (Interactive workbook)

_____. *Experiencing God: How to Live the Full Adventure of Knowing and Doing the Will of God*. Nashville: Broadman & Holman, 1994. (Trade book)

Bounds, E. M. *Power through Prayer.* Grand Rapids: Baker, 1992.

Brandt, Henry and Kerry L. Skinner. *The Heart of the Problem: A Prescription for a Deeper Experience with God.* Nashville: Broadman & Holman, 1995. (Interactive workbook)

———. *The Heart of the Problem.* Nashville: Broadman & Holman, 1996. (Trade book)

Chambers, Oswald. *Approved unto God.* Fort Washington, Pa.: Christian Literature Crusade, 1991.

———. *If You Will Ask.* Fort Washington, Pa.: Christian Literature Crusade, 1985.

———. *My Utmost for His Highest.* Nashville: Thomas Nelson, 1994.

Duewel, Wesley L. *Measure Your Life.* Grand Rapids: Zondervan.

Forsyth, P. T. *The Soul of Prayer.* Vancouver, London: C. H. Kelly, 1916.

Guyon, Madame Jeanne. *Experiencing God through Prayer.* Springdale, Pa.: Whitaker House.

Hallesby, O. *Prayer.* Minneapolis: Augsburg, 1994.

Hession, Roy and Revel. *The Calvary Road.* Fort Washington, Pa.: Christian Literature Crusade, 1973.

Hunt, T. W. *The Mind of Christ: The Transforming Power of Thinking His Thoughts.* Nashville: Broadman & Holman, 1995.

Hunt, T. W. and Claude V. King. *The Doctrine of Prayer.* Nashville: Convention Press, 1986.

———. *In God's Presence.* Nashville: LifeWay Press, 1995.

———. *The Mind of Christ.* Nashville: LifeWay Press, 1994. (Interactive workbook).

———. *PrayerLife: Walking with God.* Nashville: LifeWay Press.

Hunter, John E. *Finding What's Missing.* Kingsport, Tenn.: Fresh Springs, 1995.

———. *Knowing God's Secrets.* Kingsport, Tenn.: Fresh Springs, 1995.

Lloyd-Jones, Martyn. *Revival.* Wheaton: Crossway, 1987.

Jowett, J. H. *The Preacher, His Life and Work.* New York: Doubleday, Doran, 1928.

Murray, Andrew. *The Inner Life.* Springdale, Pa.: Whitaker House, 1984.

———. *Humility.* Springdale, Pa.: Whitaker House, 1982.

Ravenhill, Leonard. *America Is Too Young to Die.* Minneapolis: Bethany House, 1979.

———. *Revival Praying.* Minneapolis: Bethany House, 1962.

———. *Why Revival Tarries.* Minneapolis: Bethany House, 1979.

Tozer, A. W. *Knowledge of the Holy.* San Francisco: HarperCollins, 1992.

———. *The Pursuit of God.* Camp Hill, Pa.: Christian Publications, 1995.

The Pastor/Leader and His Ministry

Blackaby, Henry T. *What the Spirit Is Saying to the Churches.* Atlanta: Home Mission Board, 1988.

Blackaby, Henry T. and Claude V. King. *Fresh Encounter: God's Pattern for Revival and Spiritual Awakening.* Nashville: LifeWay Press, 1993. (Interactive workbook).

———. *Fresh Encounter: Experiencing God through Prayer, Humility, and a Heart-felt Desire to Know Him.* Nashville: Broadman & Holman, 1996. (Trade book)

Baxter, Richard. *The Reformed Pastor.* London: SCM, 1956.

Bounds, E. M. *Power through Prayer.* Grand Rapids: Baker, 1992.

Brandt, Henry. *Breaking through from the Bondage of Sin.* Eugene, Oreg.: Harvest House, 1994.

Brandt, Henry and Kerry L. Skinner. *The Heart of the Problem: A Prescription for a Deeper Experience with God.* Nashville: Broadman & Holman, 1995. (Interactive workbook)

———. *The Heart of the Problem.* Nashville: Broadman & Holman, 1996. (Trade book)

Chadwick, Samuel. *If You Will Ask.* Grand Rapids: Revell.

———. *The Way to Pentecost.* Fort Washington, Pa.: Christian Literature Crusade, 1985.

Coleman, Robert E. *Dry Bones Can Live Again.* Old Tappan, N.J.: Revell, 1969.

Culpepper, C. L. *The Shantung Revival.* Atlanta: Home Mission Board, 1982.

Drummond, Lewis. *Eight Keys to Biblical Revival.* Grand Rapids: Bethany House.

Duewel, Wesley. *Mighty Prevailing Prayer.* Grand Rapids: Zondervan, 1990.

———. *Revival Fire.* Grand Rapids: Zondervan, 1995.

———. *Touch the World through Prayer.* Grand Rapids: Zondervan, 1989.

Greenfield, John. *Power from on High: The Two Hundredth Anniversary of the Great Moravian Revival, 1726–1927.* Atlantic City: World Wide Revival Prayer Movement, 1931.

Hession, Roy. *When I Saw Him.* Fort Washington, Pa.: Christian Literature Crusade, 1992.

Huegel, F. J. *The Ministry of Intercession.*

Jowett, J. H. *The Preacher, His Life and Work.* New York: Doubleday, Doran, 1928.

McConkey, James. *The Threefold Secret of the Holy Spirit.* Philadelphia: Silver, 1897.

Mueller, George. *Answers to Prayer.* Chicago: Moody Press.

Murray, Andrew. *With Christ in the School of Prayer.* Springdale, Pa.: Whitaker House, 1981.

Olford, Stephen F. *Heart Cry for Revival.* Rev. ed. Memphis: Encounter Ministries, 1987.

Orr, J. Edwin. *Campus Aflame.* Glendale Calif.: Regal Books, 1971.

Roberts, Richard Owen. *Revival.* Wheaton: International Awakening Press, 1991.

———. *Salvation in Full Color.* Wheaton: International Awakening Press, 1994.

The Pastor/Leader and His Preaching

Duewel, Wesley. *Revival Fire.* Grand Rapids: Zondervan, 1995.

Edwards, Brian. *Revival: A People Saturated with God.* Presbyterian & Reformed, 1990.

Forsyth, P. T. *The Soul of Prayer.* Grand Rapids: Eerdmans, 1960.

Lloyd-Jones, Martin. *Revival.* Wheaton: Crossway, 1987.

Miller, Donald G. *Fire in Thy Mouth.* Nashville: Abingdon, 1954.

Orr, J. Edwin. *Campus Aflame.* Glendale, Calif.: Regal, 1971.

Owens, Ron and Patricia. *Return to Me: A Fresh Encounter with God through Song.* Nashville: LifeWay Press, 1993.

Ravenhill, Leonard. *America Is Too Young to Die.* Minneapolis: Bethany House, 1979.

———. *Revival Praying.* Minneapolis: Bethany House, 1962.

———. *Why Revival Tarries.* Minneapolis: Bethany House, 1979.

Stewart, James A. *A Faith to Proclaim.* Asheville, N.C.: Revival Literature.

Scripture Index

Subject Index

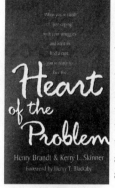

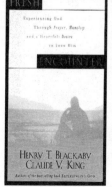

...More Insights For
Your Ministry

The Insights For Ministry Collection

Creating Community • *Dr. Glen S. Martin & Dr. Gary L. McIntosh*

In an age of change and uncertainty, small group fellowships provide the support and care that no other source can offer. *Creating Community* contains valuable advice for starting and nurturing a small group ministry. Written by two leading experts on church growth, this book gives congregations both the will and the skill to become effective witnesses in this dynamic form of ministry.

0-8054-6100-0

Effective Evangelistic Churches • *Thom Rainer*

Part research project, part detective story, this book presents results from the most comprehensive study of successful churches in history. These 586 churches across America excel in winning new souls for Christ, and have a remarkable range of things in common. Some stereotypes are shattered, some results are astonishing, and everything is written in readable, non-technical style.

0-8054-5402-0

Revitalizing The Sunday Morning Dinosaur • *Ken Hemphill*

Some church leaders consider Sunday School to be a tired old dinosaur. But according to church growth expert Ken Hemphill, Sunday School is not only still relevant, it's the key to integrated church growth for the next century. In *Revitalizing the Sunday Morning Dinosaur,* Dr. Hemphill describes how a well-crafted Sunday School program can propel any church to new levels of growth and outreach.

0-8054-6174-4

Putting An End To Worship Wars • *Elmer Towns*

In searching for the most meaningful form of worship, congregations sometimes find differences that tear them apart. Church leaders fear worship wars, and rightly so. This book explains that there are numerous approaches to worship, all biblically and culturally appropriate. The result is that everyone gains a new appreciation for differing styles within a context of courtesy, selflessness, and a willingness to listen to opposing views.

0-8054-3017-2

AVAILABLE AT FINE CHRISTIAN BOOKSTORES EVERYWHERE

The Bridger Generation
Thom S. Rainer

The Bridger Generation is the first comprehensive study of the new generation, 72 million strong, born between 1977 and 1994. These are "the Bridgers" who will be the first generation to come of age in the twenty-first century, bridging the gap between two centuries and two millennia. Rainer's in-depth analysis explores and explains revealing data, facts, and trends about tomorrow's leaders and how best to present them with the gospel of Jesus. Moving beyond the Baby Boomers, Busters, and Generation X, *The Bridger Generation* takes a unique first look at the next American demographic phenomenon.

0-8054-6296-1

The Empowered Leader
Ten Steps to Servant Leadership
Calvin Miller

Best-selling author Calvin Miller examines the seeming contradiction in the biblical concept of servant leadership: that only the obedient are worthy to command others. He then explores 10 keys to becoming a servant leader, using King David as a model. Includes contemporary observations and reflections on wisdom and compassion in leadership.

0-8054-1098-8

In The Lion's Den

A Shocking Account Of Persecution & Martyrdom Of Christians Today and How We Should Respond   *Nina Shea*

More Christians have died for their faith in the 20th century than in the previous nineteen centuries combined. This book documents the persecution of Christians in China, Pakistan, Saudi Arabia, and other countries, examining the reasons why American churches have remained silent on such a critical issue. A special section offers specific suggestions for action to raise the awareness level of religious persecution, and encourage authorities around the world to let Christians worship and teach in peace.   0-8054-6357-7

Church Administration Handbook

Revised Edition

Bruce P. Powers, Editor

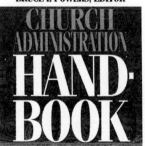

BRUCE P. POWERS, EDITOR

The original has been heralded as one of the most helpful tools in print for church leaders and administrators. Now this newly revised and updated edition offers even more practical administrative guidelines, organizational hints, advice on personnel matters and much more. Together with the newly revised *Christian Education Handbook*, this volume

A REVISED AND COMPLETELY UPDATED EDITION

provides complete basic church information and administrative guidelines.   0-8054-1061-9

AVAILABLE AT FINE CHRISTIAN BOOKSTORES EVERYWHERE